BOOMERS AND GEEZERS (Almost) SURVIVAL GUIDE

Ben Swilley

ISBN: 1481259776
ISBN-13: 9781481259774

Visit Ben Swilley's Blog at geezergrit.com

BOOMERS AND GEEZERS
(Almost)
SURVIVAL GUIDE

Why (Almost)? The Fountain of Youth is still lost. Our immortality seems doubtful.

These whimsical, humorous anecdotes were written by an old geezer for boomers and other old geezers. Share funny, off-the-wall accounts of our quirky and crazy lives. Discussed here are humorous events, strange maladies and curious ailments we have suffered for over 60 years.

This is a look ahead for boomers or anyone heading down that slippery slope to geezerdom. You better take a quick look because that is how it happens....quick. Lightning would be faster if it didn't zigzag! This book is also for those of you who have chosen to live with us. You have witnessed and endured our metamorphosis from fairly good people to unbearable grouches. God bless you all!

As a point of reference, Boomers are the folks that think someone still cares if they stand around and groan and complain about everything. Geezers are older and wiser. Geezers are more submissive to their womenfolk. They rarely drive cars anymore and they take more naps.

About the Author

Ben Swilley is a 71 year old misfit. He was born in Albany, deep in the southwest corner of the state of Georgia in the area known as Sowega. In his prolific career consisting of the things you do when you are trying to grow up, he has dug ditches, worked in construction, warehousing, juke joints, roadhouses and honkey-tonks. In recent years he has successfully managed a number of mid-sized trucking companies and he has been digging some more ditches. He currently resides in Athens, Georgia with his lovely wife, Kay, and although he has failed miserably at growing up, he has learned to be much more obedient in his old age.

Foreword

For the past few years I have struggled with a myriad of ailments that I frequently refer to as "Old Man Miseries." So far I have avoided the battle with the Big "C" with the exception of a few places on my face caused by hanging out on the coast at Panama City Beach, Florida too much when I was a kid. Otherwise, I have all the Old Man Miseries. The cost of my misspent youth now allows me no rain checks from the payback of daily aches and pains.

I have become convinced the only remedy that truly works on a fairly consistent basis each and every day is for me to drag out of bed and immediately find something that makes me laugh or smile. This always seems to side track the pain. I believe if you try this approach you can sometimes win the battle and even lose the pain completely for a while.

Research shows you can laugh your pain away. If you can expose yourself to humorous happenings and take time to join friends for laughs and giggles, they say your pain threshold becomes higher and you increase your capacity to handle the pain.

Those days when you can spend some time laughing and being happy are the best days. Most often you are the only one who can make them happen.

The stories in this book are full of tall tales and unabashed embellishments because it makes me happy to write them this way. Sometimes the tales are awfully tall and it takes much more than a grain of salt to digest them. I often laugh at what I have written and the more laughter I can produce from my befuddled mind, the better I feel.

I hope you enjoy this book. I hope it makes you laugh.

Table of Contents

I – STAYING YOUNG IN ATHENS

Katie Mae and I are from Albany in Southwest Georgia. Employment opportunity for me had us living in the Southeastern part of the state in Statesboro, Georgia for over eleven years. We had no relatives there and visits from friends and loved ones were few and far between.

We moved to Athens, Georgia from Statesboro at the end of August, 2012. We have a son who lives near Athens in Watkinsville and we have a nephew who has a lovely wife and two fine young sons who live in Athens. We were always totally aware that other relatives and friends would be eager to visit us during football season if we lived in Athens.

We felt we would benefit from exposing our aging selves to the youthful experiences that occur so often each day in Athens. Not only has our appraisal of the benefits of the move to Athens proved to be true but we left the oppressive heat of South Georgia behind and, last but never least, there ain't no gnats in Athens.

Athens, Georgia – Getting Here and Getting Younger

Moving to Athens taught me my back can now hurt in five different places. That's two more places than it had previously hurt. That's just my back. I hate to mention arthritic knees, painful hands and feet and a head that feels like it's three times bigger than a prizewinning pumpkin. I am proud that while moving, I held the number of my curses to pretty much the same level as always and my saying bad words did not worsen so that's a good thing. I keep trying to work on my vocabulary and to cut out the really bad words I use but it's a tough change to make. We lived on a golf course in Statesboro, Georgia where a lot of Georgia Southern University students played the game and I was sometimes depressed to hear the same old bad four-letter words over and over from the young duffers. I thought about writing a letter to the editor of the paper and suggesting Georgia Southern start a class for all us blue streak cussers. We could make up new words for the old ones but I guess that would be too much of a change for a fine old educational institution. I'm proud that Kay has a euphemism for BS that goes like this: "Bull-Horsey" in a loud, forceful voice. Instead of saying bull s**t or horse s**t, she just shouts "Bull-Horsey" and that covers the whole gamut. What's funny is that people seem to automatically understand what she means. Even better was an expression my old friend Ervin Lindsay used. Ervin was a religious fellow and when the urgent need would arise for a good colorful expression, old Ervin would yell, "gotta tomato nose!" This was a great substitute for "God a Mighty Knows." It suited us well and sometimes I still use "gotta tomato nose!"

In Statesboro, Kay was a volunteer in the gift shop at East Georgia Regional Medical Center and one afternoon she brought home a gift for me. It was a frog about two feet tall with skin like green velvet. I know frogs don't have velvety green skin but, what the hell, they can't sing like Satchmo either. This frog can sing. If you mash a little red spot on his hand, he will sing "What a Wonderful World" just like old Satchel Mouth. I named the frog Frank. He was definitely not Kermit but he looked a lot like Kermit so I thought Kermit might have a brother named Frank. Frank is fairly formal. He always wears a stiff white collar (no shirt) and a pink necktie with baby blue polka dots. He always has a straw hat that looks more like the one your grandmother used to wear outside on week days. It should be a properly fitted bowler but Frank came from China and what do the Chinese know about gentlemen or frogs wearing bowlers? On Friday evenings, in Statesboro, we would have a bar in the kitchen laden with hors d'oeuvres so we could have delicious snacks with our fresh peach daiquiris. I would get Frank out of the closet and sit him on a bar stool next to me. He was the world's greatest drinking buddy. He was a cheap date. He never took the first drink and he let me do all the talking. Once in a while if a subject became boring or depressing I could reach over, grab old Frank by the hand, press the red button and let him sing to me about this wonderful world we live in. What a pal!

Unfortunately, I had to cut way back on drinking anything but water and Frank was relegated to a lonely spot on a shelf in our closet.

As Katie Mae and I finally settled into this new home and the worst kind of weariness seized us by all the bones in our tortured frames, we bumped into each other in the closet one day and as I backed off a bit, I discovered I was in the closet with this beautiful woman I have been married to for so many wonderful years and since we both seemed to be too tired to talk, I spotted old Frank sitting on a shelf in a new closet in a new town and I was compelled to reach up and squeeze the red spot on his left hand. He began croaking "What a Wonderful World" to us. I grabbed Katie Mae and we danced in the new closet in the new house in Athens, Georgia with a green velvety frog serenading us. Who could ask for more?

Now we have created a little shrine for Frank. He sits on the top of a small bookcase in my office. He has an adorable picture of Miss Piggy on the wall next to his head (we know Miss Piggy belongs to Kermit but Frank can still dream, can't he?) and our old friend Snoopy is standing there with him. Snoopy has on his green scout's hat with the red neckerchief. Together we are all growing younger in Athens.

An Athens Aerobic Attempt

We thought we were ascending some pretty steep hills when we would go for walks in our other two favorite Georgia towns of Albany and Statesboro. Little did we know that Athens has mountain like hills. Now I realize that before we came here we were living in the flatlands of Georgia. When we lived south of the gnat line, I estimated we were walking a 15 minute mile but just before we moved from Statesboro, I began to use an application on my iPhone that put the lie to my calculations. Big Sister is inside the iPhone. She is watching our every feeble step. She talks to me. She makes complimentary comments on each milepost we reach. I don't know who set the mileposts but they are recognized by Big Sister each time you hit one. With a syrupy, cheerful babble she tells you how great you are doing and it doesn't faze her one bit if I say, "Shut up, you phony bitch, my feet are killing me." My legs feel like burning logs and my lungs hurt like I just lit up the last cigarette of the fourth pack for the day. But it's wonderful that you can set the app so there is applause if you actually stumble around and walk over a half mile. Let me tell you, it does not sound like sincere applause to me. It sounds cynical and pretty damned sarcastic to my way of thinking.

Anyhow the app is by Nike and it is nosy. It's already spying on you but it can't resist the chance to be even nosier. It wants you to manually verify the kind of shoes you are wearing. I lied and punched in Nike Air Max. I have no idea if there is a shoe named Nike Air Max but I saw that icon on the screen and used it out of fear a satellite-generated lightning bolt would burn my feet off at the ankles. I'm wearing Reeboks (two of them) with the DMX construction that I love so much. The DMX shoe occasionally returns some semblance of feeling to my feet and I am appreciative even if the feeling is a stabbing ice pick like plunge into the center of a big toe.

Anyhow we set off down the street to the west. This is all downhill and it is pretty much a breeze. Katie Mae is a short gal and I almost always have the advantage of the longer stride unless my lungs begin feeling like they're hanging out my nostrils and I notice my hands are purple. Then I cut her some slack. Katie Mae is making strange little mincing steps and when I question her about her odd gait, she says the hill is so steep her shoe tops are rubbing her toes so hard she is afraid her toenails will pop off. Now this worries me because recently I've noticed my toenails thickening on one foot and after a good doctor described this as fungus, I read that the fungus can cause your toenails to pop off. I wondered if they would pop off with little explosions. Would they rip out the top of your shoe and cut the leg of a bystander? Would they slice through the neighbor's mail box post?

So here we are, both of us, taking little delicate mincing girly steps down the street when we encounter a problem worse than free flying toenails. Katie Mae is deathly afraid of bugs. This sometimes works to my advantage when she leaps into my arms if a roach walks by. Unfortunately, for me, we had no bugs in our Statesboro house. We saw one roach in over 11 years and he was in that "leaving this life" pose with his little arms and legs frozen in a heavenward plea for redemption. I guess they have arms and legs. If you look closely you can see their little fingers and toes. Anyhow, we have walked just a few yards when we see dozens of wasps swarming around spots on the sidewalk. This makes walking difficult for me because this short woman is bobbing and weaving like a prizefighter around these wasps who show absolutely no interest in us. It doesn't matter. She is afraid of them and we continue our odd stilted strut around the cul-de-sac at the end of the street in a strange apoplectic dance of the zombies. I can sense the neighbors are nervously peering from behind drawn curtains. This is a quiet neighborhood. I never see neighbors but I am sure they are watching us dance like drunken loons across the cul-de-sac and then they see us fall into our desperate crawl up the ascending mountaintop on the far side of the street. I'm saying a little prayer that the neighbors will think we are practicing for a "Dance of the Dead" Halloween performance. Luckily the wasps do not appear on the shaded side of the street so our only formidable foe is the sharp incline before us.

We have to make this circuit three times. I have a band that goes around my chest that listens to my heartbeat and it tells a watch on my wrist how my pulse is faring. It sometimes scares the hell out of me when the watch shows a blank face. I know death is imminent but I somehow manage to drag in that next ragged breath of salvation and I hear the watch laughing maniacally and a tiny voice whispers, "Gotcha!"

We hope we are now familiar with houses where all the large dogs live. Katie Mae was bitten by a big dog when she was a child so we have to fight that fear too. I think she is getting tougher and better but when two Shetland-pony sized German Shepherds come around the corner of a house in full Coon Dog baying mode, I become the one with a problem as the numbers on the wrist watch began to fluctuate wildly and my feeble mind sends me into an old-fashioned swoon. When I regained my composure, it took me thirty minutes to find her. She was six houses down and across the street in someone's backyard. She was four feet up in a Bartlett Pear tree. Katie Mae was okay but the neighbor is still mad about the bark and limbs missing from the tree.

When it all ended we had walked 2.78 miles in 49.26 minutes. We were doing a 17 minute 45 second mile. That's not too bad for old folks. I think I lost some time getting her out of that tree but her time had to be better than mine because those short legs didn't seem to slow her down when she left me alone with those big German Shepherds.

Not only did we get a large round of insincere applause from the Nike Big Sister but she also put a gal with an Australian accent on the phone who told us how wonderfully we had performed. They must have missed the part where Katie Mae left the course. Now that I know Big Sister is watching, I always put my phone face down when I'm not using it and I never take it into the bathroom with me.

I rewarded myself last night with two large brownies warmed in the microwave and covered in four scoops of vanilla ice cream. The Nike gal said I had lost 325 calories and at my age you really have to be careful. It's tough keeping your weight up when you get old.

Game Day – Staying Young in Athens

It's the night before the game. We have house guests. We tell outlandish lies. We laugh a lot. It's good to laugh a lot. You can smell the endorphins forming in the laughter-filled air of the room. The pain in your old and mostly worn out body has either diminished or completely vanished. It is a great time. The younger group drinks quickly in a rush to kill their own definition of pain and misery. The two old liars are no longer imbibers of adult drinks. They might as well be sucking on binky nipples but they are accomplished guffawers and knee slappers and maintain a steady stream of psycho-babble that usually entertains nobody but just the two of them.

We listen to Paul's CD. He has had five or six songs recorded by a studio downtown and they sound more professional than the recordings he had made in years past. He is a crooner and he brings tears to the girls' eyes. He sings an old Irish folksong, "Carrickfergus," and we all have to wipe our eyes. He has to stop singing because he is turning the happy booze into sad blues. The young ones drink a little more but we all turn in early.

The dashing, daring younger women are out the door first the next morning. They are tailgating in a parking deck somewhere near Sanford Stadium and we are going to see our wonderful nephews and gorgeous niece at "Swilleygate" at the foot of the stadium, behind the Tate Center and almost under the bridge. We have Rose and Katie Mae and O.Victor with us and Paul as our wheel man. Paul has lived here about 15 years and with him driving, I feel better about navigating the madness of traffic jammed by hundreds of other lost souls trying to find a place to park. O.Victor and I marvel at the thriftiness of today's young women. We know the economy is bad and cloth is expensive but the incredible ability of these girls to cover so much with so little is heartwarming. We really appreciate the sacrifices our young college women are making. We did not pay much attention to the young guys. I guess they have their clothing costs and money problems too but I feel sure they'll be okay.

Since O.V. has back problems and the girls would rather not walk too far, Paul drops them off about a block from our destination. Victor has a couple of small insulated bags he insists on carrying for the girls. These bags are the size designed for a six pack of beer or soda so I know they can't be very heavy but I also know that his back is not that reliable and I can see a problem developing. Paul and I continue to our parking deck. We have a cooler with wheels and a couple of camp chairs we bring with us after we have parked and started out for Swilleygate.

We were about two blocks from the stadium and I become increasingly worried as we approached the back of the Tate Center. We saw Swilleygate and all the happy participants but we saw no Katie Mae, no Rosie, and no O.Victor. We had walked at least twice the distance the girls and Vic had to navigate and they were not there.

Paul ventured out on a sortie to rescue them. He had gone only about a hundred yards when he found Katie Mae and Rose. They were fuming. They claimed we let them out of the car too far from the stadium. I think they walked in circles. When you become angry and start seeing red, it's easy to lose your bearings and to walk in circles. Their big problem was our fearless leader, O.Victor. When they strapped those saddle bags (he insisted he could carry) on him, his normal snail pace slowed to a shuffle that moved him slightly forward (about three inches) every step he took. Paul says when he finally found Uncle Vic, he was moving so slowly a passing turtle was urinating on Vic's foot.

You cannot begin to believe how much bitching we were subjected to after this little episode. Vic says he told them to go ahead and he would find his way. Rose says she was worried about him falling over dead so she kept walking back and forth between him and Kay so he wouldn't be permanently lost. Kay says her method was best. She was only about a block ahead of them and before she made a turn she would wave at Vic and point in the direction she intended to take. It was good that we were in the land of plenty. Andrea and Britt always have a great amount of food and drink available and once we got to stuffing food into grumbling mouths, things quieted down. I was just so glad Paul found Vic. If he hadn't found him, people leaving the game after it was over would surely have trampled old Vic while he was still inbound to Swilleygate.

There is much of the Fountain of Youth to be found in Athens on game day. It's contagious and it flows straight from pools of excitement seen in the eyes of countless young people having so much marvelous and awesome fun. The UGA Redcoat Marching Band is only 50 feet or so in front of us and they begin to ramp up all that excitement tenfold. The drums bring the thrill of it all straight to your heart in an ever rising crescendo. This first form of primitive communication can still bind us all together into a single-minded group of happy warriors with thousands of voices booming out as a single gargantuan call to arms.........."GOOOOOO DAWWWGGGSSS!!"

The dashing, daring, younger women, K.K. and Bonnie arrive at Swilleygate just in time for the Dawg Walk. The band has now formed parallel lines stretching across the back of The Tate Center all the way back down to Lumpkin Street on one end and to the stadium on the other. Here come the Bulldogs! Bonnie and K.K. are right at the forefront with all the other Dawg lovers, yelling and screaming words of love, admiration and encouragement. They're slapping the players on their backs, their waists, their butts, and any other piece of a player's anatomy they can lovingly smack. The best bodily protection the team is afforded is the band's trombone section where the slinging slides and tossing heads of the trombone players put up a formidable defense for the helpless players. Fortunately none of them are seriously injured by the adoring crowd and they eventually play an excellent winning game against Vanderbilt. As soon as the players have passed through the Dawg Walk line, two of the members of the band climb the steps to the third floor landing outside the Tate Center and begin their famous Rooster cheer. The crowd repeats each line of the cheer and they wind it all up with the Rooty Toot Toot calling of the Bulldogs. The excitement then begins to transfer to inside the stadium for the start of the game.

The dashing and daring gals go in to see the game. We don't see them again until around midnight. They loyally watched the entire game even though it was a Georgia Bulldog rout. After the game, when they finally reached their car, the police made them go an unfamiliar route. They got lost and it took them a while to get back home.

We return to Swilleygate and feasted as the game began. We have grown older so we don't attend the games often. The restroom facilities and the food and conveniences all happen to be right where we are and so it suits us fine to visit with our younger kin. Often folks from Albany and old friends from other towns we have lived in will stop by to say hello. Britt and Andrea have been hosting "Swilleygate" since 2003. They do a wonderful job and the place has become a magnet for old and new friends and especially younger kinfolks. They also have two amazing sons who happen to be large, loving, caring lads (John and Thomas) who do not mind bending down and picking up old uncles who tend to topple over from time to time. This is one of the reasons we moved to Athens.

As I said, the excitement is contagious and it will rejuvenate you, body and soul. Be a spectator at such an event.

Ben Swilley

Go watch Georgia play football in Athens. All those young people are going to put you as close to the Fountain of Youth as you will ever get. It's reminiscent of falling in love again.

Russ is Uga -The Real Deal – Athens, Georgia, Sept. 2012

I couldn't help but notice that our old friend from Southwest Georgia, K.K. Snyder, had a Facebook post this afternoon from "Between the Hedges." It's a cartoon photo of my main man, Snoopy, perched atop his house while typing out a note on his typewriter. The note reads, or so it says, "Russ is UGA IX. Darn Good Dawg." I had to help Snoopy out a little bit and fix it here because he had a capital "U" in UGA but he had lower case letters for the "G" and the "A". What does he know? Hell, he's a dog! What's more, it must be terribly uncomfortable to type while sitting up on the sharp peaked roof of a dog house. He never seems to notice! When you stay in as much trouble as Snoopy and I do, a numb ass just can't be beat. What's even more, Snoopy has fewer fingers with which to type and he does it all on an old manual typewriter. He could, no doubt, use a computer but Shultz was stingy. He made a fortune on Snoopy and old Snoop has no running water and no electricity for the world's favorite dog. Just a couple of days ago I was so glad we had finished unpacking and sticking our heads in packing boxes and pulling out junk and more junk that I decided to take a stroll around the neighborhood. The hood is beautiful. There is a long street that goes down a pretty steep hill for over half a mile, it hits a cul-de-sac, turns around and then comes right back past you again. This has got to be the quietest neighborhood in America. After two weeks, I have seen only a couple of kids far down at the cul-de-sac and three or four adult-type human beings wandering around, at a distance.

So I put on a nice tee shirt with no holes, some fairly passable cargo shorts, and my favorite go-aheads. That's Eddie Middleton talk for sandals. He says the kind I wear have no heels so you can't back up in them, you have to go-ahead. For one last time, I go to the basement and pull out a box and rip out about 50 neckties. I found the one I needed pretty fast. Most of you probably don't remember but when Snoopy wears shades, he becomes "Joe Cool." My tie is black and white and covered with images of Snoopy in sunglasses. The only colors on the tie are the preppy sweaters Snoopy is wearing and on every sweater, it says, "Joe Cool." I put on the tie. I don't have to worry about sunglasses. Mine turn pitch black in the sun. I can't even see my feet and I wear a size 14 go-ahead.

I'm so happy to be in Athens and to be free from packing and unpacking boxes full of junk and free from mowing and yard work. I'm so happy that I start to dance down the sidewalk. The thing I'm most thankful to be free of is "GNATS." There are no gnats in Athens. That's why I'm here.

I remember seeing Snoopy doing a happy dance on Schroeder's piano as Schroeder played and Lucy listened and then they angrily stared poor Snoopy down as he wilted and crawled off stage. I love the happy dance so I improvise and I do a really bad imitation of the Snoopy happy dance. I was really slapping the sidewalk with those number 14 sandals. I got up too much momentum going down that steep hill, wheeled a few yards off course and wound up in a lady's gardenia bush three houses down.

I thought I was old. The woman who came out of the house must have been ninety. She bent over slowly and grinned at me and said sweetly, "I saw you come down that hill and bust your ass in my front yard. Just what in the hell did you think you were doing?" I smiled back at her because I'm pretty tough, and I said proudly, "I was doing the Snoopy Happy Dance No-Gnat Boogie!"

She shook her head slowly in disbelief and said, "No, No, No, No, No. What I saw you doing boy, was a simple, stupid, sad-ass shuffle."

Then she called her son outside to help me get out of her gardenia bush. He must have played football for Georgia back in the sixties because he was still a huge guy and when he saw my Snoopy tie, he said, "What you got on that dumb dog tie for?" I said, "Wait a minute man, Snoopy is the greatest dog in the world!" He said, "No he ain't. Russ is the greatest dog in the world. He's just been named UGA IX."

I may not be able to dance but I can sense imminent danger and bodily harm (especially to my own body) so I thought for a second and said, "What's your name?" He said, "Russ." I said, "Oh." I thought for another second and then said, "Listen Russ, you've got to do some real thinking.... with a degree of distinction here." Russ frowned and said, "Are you saying I smell bad?" I hurriedly replied, "Oh, no, no, I mean you need to distinguish between a real dog and a make believe dog. Russ is the real deal! Why hell man, Snoopy is a cartoon dog!"

Russ said, "Oh," and as he was busy thinking about dawgs and distinctions, I crawled back up that steep hill to my house.

Sometime after I had written this, I was corrected many, many times by UGA and Uga fans who are in the know. Snoopy was right. The correct and proper name for Russ is Uga. The University is the only entity, living or not, that is referred to as UGA.

Athens – Outlet Malls and Loud Music

The outlet malls are not in Athens. They are in Commerce but I had to make a conscious effort to leave Athens in order to drive to Commerce. That wasn't easy for me because I am rarely conscious. Katie Mae says I sleep all the time. I told her I once read an article that told me relaxation can control seizures and it's always worked for me. I have never had a seizure. She told me I was right about that and the only time she ever saw me look like I was having a seizure is when my snoring caused me to shudder violently.

Anyhow, after a couple of false starts (which seems to be normal behavior after you get older than sixty) we get to Commerce. As much as I enjoy shopping, my body no longer cares for it, not even a little bit. My back starts talking to me in a really rough voice about how I need to go outside to one of those metal benches and sit down and give it a rest. The problem is the benches are cold and the wind is still blowing pretty hard from that hurricane, Sandy. Who would have ever thought a gal with a cute name like Sandy would have such bad breath. She just about blew us all away.

The store that interested me most was a large consignment shop. I don't think I have ever been in a consignment shop before. It's pretty interesting to see what people bring from their homes to sell in the store. It's almost like snooping around in someone's house and passing judgment on the stuff they once thought was desirable. You get that furtive feeling like you are being sneaky, while at the same time you are thinking, "My gosh, I can't believe they had that tacky piece of junk in their house." Then you start to feel guilty about all the tacky junk you've got cluttering up the place you call home.

Of course, someone could have given that rubbish to them but I don't think so. This tacky junk had that warm, fuzzy, well-worn and well-loved look about it.

Naturally we bought some of the tacky junk. We had to have it. When we moved from Statesboro to Athens we only had 300 plus boxes of that same kind of stuff and we need to keep that volume pumped up pretty good or we'll begin to feel impoverished and that next move to the nursing home will be embarrassing. I can hear the other old people in the nursing home saying, "When they came here to the nursing home, they didn't have nothing. Everything he owned was in a shoe box and it was a woman's size five shoe box!"

The amount of junk you have accumulated makes for bragging rights when they put you in the old folk's home. If I'm still kicking, I'm going to be able to toss my head back and declare, "We had to get shed of over 300 boxes of tacky junk before they would let us come here." I'm sure everybody feels the same way as I do. You have absolutely got to own a lot of purely worthless "stuff." It makes you feel better!

I'm sorry, I got carried away. Back in the consignment store the lad at the checkout counter was overwhelmingly humorless. The sign taped to the counter said you must have a "reciept" if you are returning an item. I mentioned receipt was spelled incorrectly and I said to the boy, "I'll bet you hear that all the time?" The kid says, "Nah, that's the first time. You're the only one who's ever mentioned it." I was going to launch into the little high school English ditty about, "I before E except after C," but I had already decided the kid was a lost cause. If he had a hundred pockets in his shirt and jeans we couldn't have found a tiny piece of personality in any of them.

We paid up and left but not before I learned two things about operating a consignment shop. If you own or manage the shop you must price the items yourself because, if it is left to the owners, they will always overprice their tacky junk. The second thing he said was, "We're not taking any more clothes in on consignment until March." Today is the last day of October so that tells you something about the economy doesn't it? People are desperately trying to sell their old clothes and their junk.

At four o'clock the Halloween trick or treaters appear from every nook and crannie and we quickly leave the so-called "Outlet Mall." We get out just before being trampled by tiny action figures swinging lethal orange pumpkins made like round buckets with a big hole in the top that gives maximum access for shoveling the candy in.

I leave the mall with my normally numb head even more unfeeling and devoid of sensation. I cannot believe people who have obviously invested so much time, effort and money in a retail store would actually let the kids they employ as clerks choose the type of music they are playing to their potential customers and, what's even worse, the kids also have control of the volume switches for the tasteless music they choose.

I'm only trying to maintain any youthful vigor I might have once had. I don't really want to be young again. I certainly don't want to be young now. I do not want to be in the company of the greatest number of air-heads America has produced since I was born. The music these kids play in department stores is enough to regenerate life in the brain dead. Maybe that's a good thing. How can you possibly shop with blaring music from an alien world inhabited by beings whose eardrums are made of inch-thick teak wood?

We crossed the street and entered a Mexican restaurant. I just thought the music in the mall stores was screeching and obnoxious. From somewhere over my head a television was blasting away. It sounds like more action figures only in real true action. This time they were on the air and trying to kill each other. It must have been one of those Ultimate Fighting Competition bouts going on. You know the kind of fighting I'm talking about. This is the one watched by people who look like they're from the movie cast of "The Night of the Living Dead."

There is a chain-link fence built around the ring that looks like the protective ring around a trampoline. I don't know if the fence is to contain the fighters inside the ring or to keep the "Living Dead" out of the ring.

And then it happened. Someone on my left kicked up the volume on the Mexican music. Now I had an ultimate fight going on overhead and Mexican music threatening to destroy my mind on my left. This used to happen in my home town of Albany, Georgia. I broke them up from making that racket while I was trying to eat lunch. I would leap to my feet, scream Spanish words like tortilla, el toro and enchilado and then I would break into my version of a flamenco dance. They would send five waiters to my table at the same time. All of them would try to say simultaneously, "Pleeze Senor, we turn off all music if you pleeze, just do not dance."

Now, I cannot stand too fast or I'll get dizzy and fall over. Besides, if I don't behave, Katie Mae will throw every knife, fork and spoon on the table at me. I surrendered. I stuffed black beans in my ears, buried my face in my taco salad and suffered through it as best I could.

I don't want to be young again. I just want to shop and eat my meals in peace.

But, boy oh boy, if only I could still be big enough and mean enough to scare the hell out of belligerent kids and Mexican waiters. I would still be flamenco dancing on their tables.

Athens-UGA- Homecoming 2012 – Game Day

UGA home games are seriously bad for an old man's health. I was doing great with my weight control scheme until game day. I gained five pounds just inhaling the air around the stadium. People have tail-gating operations set up on top of other tail-gaters. They're packed so tight in some places that one guy winds up turning burgers on the other guy's grill and neither one knows the other is encroaching. Toss in a few cold beers and exotically colored girly drinks and before too long everybody is eating everybody else's food and nobody knows who prepared or cooked what, and furthermore, nobody gives a damn.

Britt and Andrea host SwilleyGate. It is set up by Britt bright and early the morning of each home game. Britt has coolers you could put a whole hog in but he has chosen to fill them with water and soft drinks to relieve the parched throats of the throngs who cheer on the Bulldogs. There are a couple of Georgia UGA tents and plenty of UGA chairs for old folks like me and four or five tables that will soon be ladened with more food than a family of ten could eat in a week. A little later, Andrea brings in small mountains of finger foods and chips and dips, sandwiches and sweets and concoctions that will soon create a shark-like feeding frenzy among the younger set. Younger folks are quicker on their feet than we are (like you didn't know that) and their elbows are sharper. They deliver near-lethal rib blows in clearing a path to the food tables. They look much like human weed-eaters as they work their way forward. I stay safely back from all the commotion but somehow I still get fat.

Friends begin showing up with more ice coolers. Did you ever think the day would come when you rolled all that liquid refreshment around right behind you in an insulated box with a telescoping handle and built-in wheels? Remember when we had to ice down all our beer in number 3 washtubs and haul them around in the bed of a pickup truck?

Now more women show up with insulated shoulder bags packed with more frilly foods and girly drinks. I never believed that old description of tables groaning but I actually heard one crying out about the weight it was carrying. Luckily the wait was short before the kids with the quicker feet and the sharp elbows lightened its load.

Homecoming is so special to so many people who, in their time of youth, were the quick of foot and the sharp of elbow. I saw one gal, in particular, who could still fit into a cheer leading outfit that looked like it was a fixture of the fifties. I'll bet she was in her seventies. She was a true sport. Later on, while viewing one of the monitors showing the game inside the Tate Student Center, I saw her on the field with a number of other cheerleaders, past and present. I can tell you, she was special and she showed it. She still made that outfit look good and, to me, she was representative of all the guys and gals who have come and gone on these revered Georgia sports fields.

The big thrill for me is when the Dawg Walk begins and the drumming begins with a rat-a-tat-tat-boom-boom-booming warm-up session that brings out the primeval in all of us. This rudimentary means of communication from the earliest days of men walking upright awakens an ancient rhythm in even the youngest of the spectators. Surprisingly the crowd grows quiet. There are few laughs or even smiles as the drums first begin their primordial message. The rapt attention on the faces of the onlookers is undeniable proof that we all are descended from ancestors, all over this world, who first expressed their innermost feelings and emotions with drum beats. It is a thrilling, chilling moment.

The primitive moment passes. The crowd relaxes and breaks into big smiles, grins, whoops and hollers as the so incredible University of Georgia Redcoat Marching Band begins to play. Spending great fortunes cannot buy you better music. They are good to the last note and the crowd really shows their appreciation. The lone trumpeter on the bridge overhead is joined by a second trumpet. I can only guess that the tradition of having a lone trumpeter is broken because today is the homecoming game. As the trumpets on the bridge lead off, the entire band begins to play as the football players begin to walk to Sanford Stadium between two parallel lines of continuously playing band members.

As soon as the players file into the stadium, two of the band members will climb the outside stairway of the Tate Student Center to the third floor landing and face the crowd below. I assume they always choose loud and rambunctious men and only those men with lungs that afford them the effortless ability to bellow like enraged Bulldawgs to the folks below.

They start off with raucous and rowdy demands on the crowd to tell them how bad the opposing team is going to play. The crowd responds with great roars. They make a couple of crowd satisfying, belittling remarks about the other team and the crowd again reacts with loud cheers.

Then they scream in unison, "Are You Ready???" The crowd goes crazy. And again, "Are You Ready??" The crowd is wild. And again, "ARE YOU READY????" There is such a reaction from the spectators that you can't be sure you will survive the onslaught. You are not even sure your heart is still beating. You can't hear anything but the noise and it carries you in a rush as if you were caught in a flash flood on a raging river.

Then they begin the most serious of all cheers:

"Had a little rooster!" the crowd repeats each stanza in an ever-increasing crescendo.

"And I put him on a fence!"

"The rooster cheered for Ole Miss."

"Because he had no sense."

"I got another rooster."

"And I put him on the fence!"

"The rooster cheered for Georgia"

"Because he had good sense!"

"I say, a Root, a Root, a Rooty Toot Toot!"

"I say, a Root, a Root, a Rooty Toot Toot!"

"GOOOOOOOOOO DAWGS!!!!"

"SIC 'EM, WOOF! WOOF! WOOF!"

You can add as many woofs as you like. I'm a three woof guy because my lungs are 70 years abused and they often rebel when called on for loud cheers.

This year I witnessed all the action from a chair at SwilleyGate. I did not brave the crowd because my feet hurt and they tend to hurt more when large clumsy, well-meaning sports fans walk on them.

It was a beautiful day. Georgia won. I was well fed. Life is good!

Thanksgiving – Katie Mae's Folks Do It All

It's unusual, it's strange, it's wild but boy does it work!!!!

We have to pack up and leave Athens to enjoy this blowout but the trip would be worth it even if we had to ride twice as far to get there.

I'm constantly amazed by the women who feed us and on this trip I have to include the bright young guys and the old Skipper who can cook. There was no written game plan. There never is! They have been putting this great event together for months before it actually happens but I never saw anything written in pencil or ink on paper. They just know how to do it and they do it right every time. The phone lines drooped from the heat of constant use by the first of the month. There was no ring leader but the phone calls kept coming and going and by the day of the big event, everybody knew what their contribution was going to be. There are a few old geezers who are slackers, like me, and who did very little, but the ever-bustling women more than made up for our innate sorriness.

It started probably ten years ago when young Kenneth Brooks (who grew up answering to the nickname, "Skeeter") began a tradition of having us over to his house for the Thanksgiving blessings. He and his lovely wife, Kimberly, are like our own children and their daughter, Kensley, most surely hung the moon, if you ask Katie Mae and me. Kimberly and Kenneth were our gracious hosts in three different homes they owned over those first five years and they are the real glue that brings us all together for Thanksgiving. The success of these fantastic gatherings is largely due to their efforts.

About five years ago a marriage in Kimberly's family gave us a wonderful connection to a great gal who owns a beautiful quail-country hunting lodge about five miles out in the woods north of Dawson, Georgia. I'm not naming names because she might be allowing us to rent it only because we have family ties.

Katie Mae and I arrived on Tuesday afternoon. Naturally we had been lost for a half hour because one of the road signs was no longer there. We are citified and the only sign we can read is the one that has colored letters and arrows on it. We have been coming out here for five years and we can't find the dirt road we need to turn down to get to the lodge. Katie Mae's brother, Jerry and his wife Alice came in from Louisiana and we were talking back and forth with them on cell phones. We passed them three times on the paved road. We kept waving as they passed us because they looked like somebody we knew. Finally we all came to our senses and stopped to ask directions from a guy who was up on the third floor of a John Deere tractor that could have buried both cars in one sweep. He left us so confused that we went ahead and found the place on our own in less than two minutes.

We bunked in at the lodge. There are three bedrooms and three baths. It has a big commercial kitchen with a tremendous great room furnished with a pool table and a wide screen television framing a huge fireplace on one end of the room with a long wet bar at the other end. There are enough tables and chairs to seat well over forty people for meals in this main room. Katie Mae's extended family can more than fill all forty chairs come Thanksgiving Day.

The strongest family connection in the entire group is the Alligood name. Just the oldest sister and the youngest sister are still with us. Two brothers and two sisters have passed away. There are children, grandchildren and great-grandchildren who, in turn, are also nephews and nieces and great nephews and great nieces and on and on. They are all blood kin to these two grand matriarchs of their respective immediate families. Katie Mae's Momma, Grace, is the oldest sister and at 90 she is still going strong. Her sister Sara is the youngest Alligood sister and she is still so active, it wears me out to watch her in action.

I have seen as many as forty-five to fifty people enjoy Thanksgiving Eve festivities at the lodge and, always, on the main event day there will be at least forty or more loving kinfolks stuffing themselves with more different foods and desserts than you can imagine or begin to name here.

Young Kenneth is a master of organization of the entire event but he really shines when it comes to the Wednesday evening festivities. Besides all the relatives there are a number of close family friends who join us on Wednesday night so the crowd can be quite large and the adjoining countryside is full of cackling and guffawing and laughter bouncing from the trunks of the great long leaf pines. Liars, story tellers and listeners circle around the huge bonfire that Ken keeps stoked by piling on wooden shipping pallets given to him by good friends just for the bonfire. I stand ready to pull intoxicated celebrants from the burning ashes if anybody falls in. That too is laughable. If one falls in he can kiss his fanny goodbye. I have grown too old to snatch drunks out of a fire.

I have never counted the number of grills and cookers these young lads fire up on Thanksgiving Eve but I can promise you there is always more food on the table than the revelers can ever possibly consume. The biggest grill is laden with venison backstrap that usually has been marinated in Ken's secret cider-marinade recipe and then wrapped in bacon. It is a true, successful hunter's version of filet mignon and there is more than enough for everyone. "Melts in your mouth" is an old timeworn expression but no other can adequately describe the tenderness of the venison. The young men show signs of a primitive and wolf-like behavior by slicing off a good chunk of meat from one of the tenderloins and then retreating to a safe spot around the bonfire. They cast age-old furtive glances in all directions lest another hungry young man-wolf is lurking in the shadows ready to challenge them for their meal. But all is well. Everybody had a shot at the deer meat and there were no fights over food.

The young Skipper and his beautiful "Bride to be," Brie, came up from South Florida with a treat that soon had a crowd gathering around his cooker. He fried some of the best red snapper I have ever eaten. It was hard not to grab a piece of the freshly fried fish and instantly pop it into your mouth while it was still sizzling. There were too many youngsters who would jockey for position around the food and they were much quicker than me. I had to show them what an old fat hip can do when you are maintaining your dominant position in the circle. Unfortunately I was too successful at getting to the fish. It took my mouth three or four days to heal after I burned off all the tender skin from inside my cheeks.

There was a huge mix of drinkers: Wine drinkers, beer drinkers and the rest of us who were barely in the race because of our age. We were reduced to strange adult concoctions and rose- colored girly drinks. I can't begin to tell you how much beer was consumed by the younger crowd. I can't believe we ever guzzled that many suds in our youth but I guess we did. Aunt Sharon and I each brought our own delectable versions of Bloody Mary mix. Every year we have to brag on our own Bloody Mary blend and we try to conspire against each other by going to various family members and asking, not-so-subtly, "Whose Bloody Mary mix do you think is the best?" The person being queried has to be careful that only one of us is in hearing distance because it is not wise to brag on one mix if the other mixer is within earshot! The funny thing is that both mixes usually taste pretty much the same and after a couple of mornings of drinking Bloody Marys, neither Sharon nor I can tell one mix from the other.

Laid back in a fine old rocking chair on the side porch of the lodge you have a view of a pond big enough to refer to as a lake. The view is galvanizing. You don't ever want to leave. We sometimes pretend to go fishing here. We pretend because real fishing is too much like work. You would have to clean them or release them and this commanding panorama is not for inspiring work but it is here for you to visually saturate your senses into a catatonic stage unattainable with alcohol or drugs. Your mind and body become one with the old rocking chair. The chair feels as if it has grown to your bottom and it is now an extension of your entire body. You thank God with all your heart because you know it just doesn't get any better than this!

Down near the lake and out of sight behind the pine trees is a building that houses flinging machines for throwing clay pigeons here, there and yonder. After the big meal on Thursday a bunch of the young shooters think they can work off the tremendous meal they just ate by shooting shotguns at helpless and defenseless clay pigeons. I hoped the pigeons were amphibious because a large number of them hit the water untouched by bird shot. The skeet shooters did much better than I could but most of them still need some serious practice. The clay pigeons were safe.

Young Cason visited us on Wednesday and I felt compelled to drag some toys out of my car so he and I could entertain ourselves while the women continued to buzz around in the lodge like crazed worker bees. Playing with toys was a big mistake on my part because I am not used to shooting slingshots and BB guns. We began to fire at low hanging pine cones to show each other how good we were at hitting the target. I tried to rapid-fire an old Daisy air rifle that had to be cocked each time you shot it. I was so good at rapid-firing the BB gun that my head and neck did not stop hurting for four days afterward which was about the same time it took for my fish-fried mouth to heal. It was a terrible pain that luckily did not attack me until Friday when we left to return to Athens. Not only did Cason out shoot me (he killed the most pine cones) but later we went inside and shot a game of pool that made me look dumber than a third grader. I'm never going to try to keep up with him again.

The main event came and went too quickly on Thursday. The pool table was commandeered by the women and a couple of the young guys brought in a plywood contrivance that, once covered with brightly colored tablecloths, transformed the pool table into the finest food serving table in the entire Southland. I could hear the plywood crying as the women arranged and placed tray after tray, pan next to pan and dish upon dish on that poor old pool table.

Skipper the Elder once again outdid himself with the turkeys. He fried three of the big birds and each one was lovingly injected with a variety of various flavors and seasonings. No two were alike and only the senior Skipper knows what he has introduced into those delicious turkeys to make them taste even better than they usually do. Skip and Sharon have lived just outside of Charleston for many years and we all are the beneficiaries of their coastal cooking skills. They always bring a Chevrolet Suburban full of food and drink for Thanksgiving.

Young Skipper sliced the turkeys. I sliced the ham. There was not a spare inch of space left on the great table.

The Alligood girls brought their two clans together in the great room of the lodge. Granny Grace and Aunt Sara joined hands with Aunt Sara's dear husband, Uncle Billy Loveless. We then all joined hands and Uncle Billy conveyed our thanks to the Lord for the feast we were about to enjoy and for the many blessings that were represented by all the fine people who gathered under that great cathedral ceiling.

Then they all merged with methodical confusion into a jostling throng that reminded me of a cross between Hurricane Sandy and the Indianapolis 500. As the crowd swarmed toward the big table, all semblance of orderliness went out the fireplace and up the chimney. People didn't quite seem to know where to start on this gargantuan spread so they started on all four corners and all four sides simultaneously. They looked like the swirling waters of a dizzying whirlpool as they flowed in and out of one line and on into the next line. I kept looking under the pool table to see if any children had been trampled. Nobody seemed to mind. Nobody tripped over anybody. They have done this for so many years that it all came naturally.

When the dust cleared, everybody had a seat and at a couple of places I saw utensils moving so fast from plate to mouth that the silverware was just a blur. I kept thinking you could really screw up your nose moving a fork that fast but nobody stabbed themselves in the frenzy and everybody was fat and happy when it was all over.

I would be so remiss if I did not say the best memory of all has to be the food traditions that are observed in the South on Thanksgiving Day. The huge pool table/serving table was totally covered with nothing but good food. At the front of the room there was a long bar built beside an equally long table that seats twelve. That long bar was also totally covered with nothing but desserts. There were pumpkin pies, pecan pies, every imaginable cake that comes to mind, banana pudding, and beautiful exotic concoctions I am afraid to try to name. I could get into much trouble with the womenfolk if I wrongfully named one of their sweet creations.

For those of you who are not from the South, I want to emphasize, just for the pleasure of self-indulgence, the memories I have of enjoying my favorite dishes that are always prepared at Thanksgiving.

The dressing is not stuffed in the breast cavity of the turkey. We do not use stuffing. We serve corn bread dressing. The dressing is made from corn meal mixed with eggs, butter, onion, and celery and the rich broth from a recently cooked hen. You absolutely have to know the difference between a fryer (broiler) and a hen if you want the right broth in your corn bread. Katie Mae adds a dozen biscuits to her dressing and she uses her own secret additions to an old recipe from Lynn Mertins. Lynn Mertins has an unequaled reputation in the preparing of culinary delights in that area of Southwest

Georgia. Her catering business is par excellence and unsurpassed. Fresh oysters from Apalachicola Bay, Florida make a dynamite addition to the dressing. Katie Mae carefully picks loose shell from each oyster and then deftly pushes the oyster into the dressing one at a time before popping the pan into the oven.

Several different versions of dressing were on the table. You cannot serve dressing without giblet gravy. The giblets (pronounced with a hard "G" like a "J." It is blasphemy to pronounce it with a soft "G.") are made up of chicken livers, gizzards and hearts of the chicken or turkey. They were chopped up with boiled eggs and more chicken stock which was added to that already produced by cooking the giblets. It is a delicious treat when lovingly ladled atop the dressing and it is, no doubt, the reason my weight, my blood sugar and my blood pressure all rise proportionately each holiday season.

All the old standard dishes round out the Thanksgiving meal and they surrounded the sliced ham and turkey in a colorful profusion of mouthwatering delicacies. There was sweet potato soufflé casserole, green bean casserole, potato salad, a seven layer salad, other layered salads, macaroni and cheese, congealed salads, butter beans, deviled eggs, chicken and dumplings, fried corn bread, zipper peas, black-eyed peas, brown rice, cranberry sauce, and last but not least was the turnip greens cooked with pork neck bones. For a double treat, the turnip greens could be eaten with cracklin' bread which is cornbread made with crisp crumbled pork rinds baked throughout the bread.

It is notably interesting that the largest and the fattest of us can so subtly (we think) maneuver our way back to the source of the food for seconds and, sometimes, for thirds. We think we are invisible. We crab-walk in a sideways slide to make ourselves look smaller. We think we are darting in and out but we are lumbering along with our heads leading our fat bottoms by a good foot or more. It's a wonder we don't fall headlong into the food platters.

It is all to die for and I'm sure meals like this account for ugly scars I have all over my body. You get scars like this when they strap you to a heart lung machine so they can swap your good veins with your totally clogged arteries and give you a second chance to enjoy the good life.

Katie Mae and I headed for Athens on Friday morning. We suffered greatly from all that fun but not like we suffered when we were younger. These days we are not hungover. She was hurting from an old eye condition that has bothered her for years. I was unable to turn my head to the left or right or up and down. I was in serious head pain. I think all that rapid-fire action with the BB gun left my neck and head paralyzed and the inside of my mouth was cooked well-done because I tried to eat a fist full of fried fish straight out of the frying pan.

So as I drove she looked to the left and right for me but I was not really sure she could see well enough to be a good navigator. We got lost a bit in Macon because we haven't driven that way to Athens in about fifteen years and I was crippled and blind and she was more than half blind.

We limped on toward home. When the two lane road widened and gave me a chance to pass a couple of Sunday drivers, I roared right on past them and met our old friend, John Law, just as we topped a hill. I went ahead and pulled over for him because it's hard to ignore those blue lights even if you feel like hell. It turns out we were in Morgan County and we had just been apprehended by one of Georgia's finest from The Department of Public Safety. After I showed him that little plastic card with my favorite picture on it and told him how great the guys are down at the insurance company I use, he had a chance to ask me if I had any particular reason for going so fast and I mentioned I was passing slower cars and that I had been driving sanely, up until that very moment. Then I laughed and said, "I'll bet you hear that a lot?" Then he laughed and said, "Yeah I do!" Then he went to his car and came back in a few minutes with a warning ticket!

Thanksgiving was stupendous and wonderful. God is great, Life is good!

Merry Christmas to Sergeant M. Meeler, Georgia State Patrol!

Christmas in Athens - 2012

I checked out the Christmas lights in downtown Athens, Georgia after dark just like I promised some old Albany, Georgia friends. We all wanted to know if Athens decorated for Christmas like Albany did in the past. The answer is a great big NO. Does any town or city decorate like Albany did in the 40's, 50's, and 60's? I don't think so.

It must have taken an incredible amount of labor to put on such a display back then. Arranging, hanging and later dismantling those decorations took many hours and many days. Apparently municipalities can no longer afford the labor or the electricity to light up the night skies of December for a colorful and joyful Christmas.

Back then the Albany lights stretched across major streets and thoroughfares and some of the displays were animated to create overhead scenes like Santa Claus in his sleigh being pulled across the street by reindeer. Other lights flashed and blinked and wished us a Merry Christmas and a Happy New Year as we drove by. Our best years are behind us. Today's young people have already been cheated of such beautiful, locally created sights. They will probably never have opportunities to enjoy the holidays like we did.

So did you have a good Christmas this year? Christmas is always the time you reflect on the Christmases you enjoyed in the past and usually those memories leave you with warm and fuzzy feelings, but not always.

I'll never forget the comb and brush set my Daddy gave me one Christmas. It is particularly memorable because I always had my hair closely clipped in what they used to call a crew cut. These days some folks call it a buzz cut. He also gave me a bottle of Vitalis hair tonic. Vitalis was a little bit cooler than the Vaseline hair tonic older guys sprinkled on their heads but those guys actually had hair that could be combed. The hair oil back then made your head greasier than a hub on the wheel of a Conestoga wagon. I had no use for any oil at all on my bur head. For a while there, after Christmas, if I happened to be in the same room with my Daddy, I would whirl around and try to catch him laughing at me or at my head. I still can't figure out why he gave me such a useless gift. He drank a little bourbon, but never enough for me to blame that strange gift on his drinking.

I particularly remember a toy violin old Santa left me one year. I might have become a virtuoso fiddler except for one small factor. There was no rosin for the bow string and with no rosin for the bow string, the violin does not emit notes or noise. I would sometimes ask my Mother or my Daddy about the chances of them hustling up a little rosin for the violin bow but Mother would give me vague answers about not knowing where to find rosin and my Daddy would get a faraway look in his eyes. Rosin is made from pine tree resin and this could not have been a huge mental challenge for either of them because you could not walk outside our South Georgia home without bumping your head on a pine limb or stubbing your toe on a pine stump.

Now I have three children of my own and I know the far-away look comes from the fright or fight reaction. The look meant my Father wanted to kill me and my Mother was only trying to save my life. He couldn't stand too much noise. Now when I think about me, the boy wonder and his wonderful violin, I'm sure it's only a dream, but I often have a clear and distinct vision of my Daddy standing at the edge of the large water filled lime sink down by our old barn and tying that little bag of rosin to a twenty pound cinder block. He then throws the block (with rosin bag attached) as far out into the water as he could chunk it. That took complete and final care of any problems a noisy violin might have caused him.

So how was your Christmas? This younger crowd thinks I am getting senile. They think I don't notice what I'm getting from them for Christmas so I have a special pay back for the ones who gave me these things: a box of old Legos; a used sweater; some dental floss that I'm pretty sure had also been used; a bug sucker that you attach to a vacuum cleaner so you can catch 'em without touching 'em. I'm the only one here who will pick up a dead roach. Thank God, we don't have many dead roaches visit us or my back would be completely whacked out. I got a belt from my cousin that I gave him two years ago for his birthday. In the last three or four years I have received seven bars of that "Soap on a Rope" stuff. I know they say you lose your sense of smell when you're getting old but has my personal hygiene gone straight to hell or what?

Last but not least, an old gal cousin of mine sent me a speedo. I don't think any guy over the age of six should wear a speedo. A guy who looks like a sack of potatoes in a knit shirt when he puts on a knit shirt should never wear knit shirts, and if he looks like that in a knit shirt, he should consider suicide before he puts on a speedo. Any fool knows you shouldn't try to stuff a sack of potatoes into a speedo!

Probably the most fun was the Christmas Eve visit to Nephew Britt and his lovely bride Andrea's new digs. It's new to them and it is new to us so we can call it "NEW" if we want to. It is a beautiful house and the folks inside the house were not only great fun to be with but their presence made us happy and the food they shared made us even happier. Andrea's Mom and Dad, Sue and Mike, were there and Britt's mom, Priscilla, was also there. She was married to my late brother Billy so that makes her my sister-in-law and that makes her wonderful son, Britt, my nephew and it makes his two wonderful sons, John and Thomas, my grand, great nephews.

Andrea and Sue had a big pot of Brunswick stew (one of my very favorites) and Katie Mae brought a big pot of chili (another one of my very favorites) and I brought Mr. Piggy's appetite with me to the party. When I finished eating, I checked out my face in a mirror and it was so fat my ears had disappeared.

The boys left us to go upstairs so Mike and I managed to tell a few old war stories as I desperately tried to get comfortable after eating all that food. In a while the boys came downstairs. They had been upstairs practicing harmonizing on a few Christmas carols.

When they came back downstairs, the greatest part of the evening commenced and that part was our being entertained by a quartet of four young guys who can literally sing like angels. Britt, John, Thomas and our son Paul sang several beautiful Christmas carols and wound up the evening with a couple of old Irish standards.

Katie Mae and Paul helped me creep fatly to the car. After stuffing myself with my very favorite foods and listening to fantastically good singing from these young guys, this just may have been my very favorite Christmas.

Happy 2013 from Athens-Dining South, New Year's Day!

It's New Year's Eve and if you have ratcheted up past the big 70 and sailed on past it another year like me, I feel pretty sure, that also like me, you're going to wear out the television screen and remote control this evening checking out the big city party action from the best seat in the house, your recliner. You might have a small token toddy just to make you feel like you're still in the game but you will be more likely to see all the action playing on the backs of your eyelids long before the big apple makes its historic descent.

I should say don't let it bother you but I already know you won't. I'm thinking of all the great grub we are going to have tomorrow because the South has an unequaled number of traditional dishes we pig out on come New Year's Day! I am remembering the traditions right now and I'm going to share them with you. You will recognize, know and love most of them just as I do but there may be a couple of surprises in here for you, just as there was for me.

Talking about a little toddy makes me want one but the acid that alcohol produces in my battered body can render me speechless so nowadays a wild week for me would involve my having dinner and consuming a total of two (almost two) twelve ounce beers with the meal. That's right. Two beers in one week! That's just on a wild week. Normally I do not, and I cannot, drink any more. I miss alcohol because it always made me happy but I would rather babble and run my mouth and old demon rum steals my voice.

Anyhow I still have a pretty good stock of the liquid gold that used to make me so happy so I went plundering for a small bottle of moonshine a friend gave me a few years back. It was stored in a little plastic water bottle. Then I remembered. The booze burned a hole in the bottle and ran out into the cabinet. It ate up half a shelf board before I noticed it. We had to have the cabinet sand-blasted. That moonshine could have put deep scars on a granite counter top. Probably it was a good thing I never tasted the stuff. I would have lost my voice a lot sooner. I remember it smelled like the expensive varnish they use to refinish yacht decks.

I tried to talk Katie Mae into buying me a bottle of Champagne Krug 1998 Clos d'Ambonnay so I could really bring in the New Year right but when I told her the bottle cost $2,200.00 she spoke harshly to me, turned out the lights and left the room. If your bride of almost 40 years refuses to answer a pure and innocent question and leaves the room as she leaves you in the dark, your New Year is starting off a trifle rocky. I thought it wise to skip any more talk about the champagne.

So here we go:

Black-eyed Peas – After the Civil War about all our folks had left to eat was black-eyed peas and greens. Northern troops destroyed most of the crops in the Old South during their invasion of God's country. The Yankees took all the food except for cowpeas (Black-eyed peas) and greens. The Yankees thought the peas and the greens were fodder for livestock and they never touched these two great food sources. This literally saved our lives and the South was reborn. Luckily we made a magnificent comeback. People who are starving to death seldom propagate.

Black-eyed peas represent coins and also dining on the peas gives us the promise of great luck and plenty of everything we need for the coming year. Some children were told to eat at least 365 peas so every day in the coming year would bring sustenance aplenty. Others were paid a visit by the "Pea Fairy" who would leave them a penny for every pea they ate. We were not that poor but I still don't remember no visit from no "Pea Fairy." To some people the peas meant friendship because peas grow in a pod and they are close together, like friends who are supposed to be as close as "two peas in a pod." Peace is also described as being a gift bestowed on black-eyed pea consumers.

A common tradition in the South is to leave three black-eyed peas on your plate uneaten. The three uneaten peas represent luck, fortune and romance. I'm going to leave two peas on my plate. I still need luck and fortune but my romance with the beautiful, sweet gal I married cannot be improved upon.

Collard Greens, Turnip Greens and Mustard Greens - You've got to have greens. Many people replace these greens with cabbage. It's all okay and it all represents money. The greens even look like folded money once it has been cooked (so they say). To me they look like collard greens, turnip greens, mustard greens or cabbage.

Greens, therefore, mean money, money, money for the entire New Year to come. Always refer to the collards, turnips and mustard as a "mess of" when you are talking about a big pot of them. I'm not sure about the cabbage. Usually you hear G.R.I.T.S. speak of a "mess of," turnips, collards or mustard. G.R.I.T.S, for those of you who don't know, stands for "Girls Raised in the South."

I have to dwell for a moment on the greens that are symbolic of our eagerly anticipated economic fortune because they are not going to be cooked to perfection if you don't put some piece of a pig in the pot with them. There are a number of pork parts you can choose to complement the greens and when I say, "complement," I mean you put the pork in the same pot with that mess of greens.

You can use hog jowls, ham hocks, a ham bone, fatback or whatever pig portion you desire but the flavor the ham gives the greens is unbeatable and unforgettable. Hog jowls are the chinny-chin-chin (sagging jaws) part of the pig and they are sometimes hard to find this time of year. Maybe hogs don't grow jowls like they used to. If you cannot guess what fatback is you have not been living a righteous life.

The fatback ensures good health and consuming any piece of the hog will bestow progress, prosperity and wealth on you in the year to come. The pig is a symbol of progress because they don't back up and always keep moving forward as they root. The hog also teaches you humility because pigs can't fly.

Skillet Cornbread - Southern skillet cornbread cannot be sweet! Many fine Southern women have drilled that admonition into us since we were old enough to eat milk and cornbread mush from a tiny bowl. Some families bake a dime in the cornbread or cook the dime in the black-eyed peas. The person who is served the dime while eating has a full year filled with a double dose of good fortune coming to her (or him).

The golden color of the skillet bread is a symbol of gold to be received for some folks. Others believe the cornbread represents humbleness. The ingredients are inexpensive so maybe that's where the "humble" part comes into play.

All I remember about cornbread, I learned from Coach Mullis and Jimmy Hall in high school geometry. Coach Mullis said, "Pie are square." Hall, who was a mathematical genius (which Coach Mullis was not) said, "No sir, Coach, pie are round. Cornbread are square." Everybody but Hall got to leave the class early that day.

I never agreed with either one of them because somehow I felt like it was all in the shape of the pan you used.

Chicken and Rice and Hoppin' John - I ran into some controversy when it comes to rice for New Year's Day. Some folks eat tomatoes and rice cooked together. The tomatoes are to ensure a healthy heart. I love this particular dish but we never eat it on the first of January. We always have chicken and rice.

Many good cooks will put the rice and the black-eyed peas together with chopped onions and sliced bacon for a delicious Southern dish known as Hoppin' John. The origin of the name is uncertain but it is believed to be a corruption of a Haitian Creole phrase for "black-eyed peas." This phrase was undoubtedly corrupted by Southern plantation owners suffering from their first and worst hangovers of the year! If Hoppin' John was served as a leftover the day after New Year's Day, it was called "Skippin' Jenny." I'll bet they got that "skippin'" part because bad hangovers would preclude most New Year's Day activities that weren't absolutely necessary.

The chicken and rice had a couple of contrasting meanings for New Year's Day. Rice was thought to stand for "purity" and to some people if you cooked the rice with chicken wings, the money would just fly into your pockets. Others contend if you cook your rice with chicken, your money will fly out of your pockets during the oncoming year. It's not hard to guess the latter group was a bunch of pessimistic old worry warts.

The only morbid belief I ran across was that you should never serve rice on New Year's Day because rice is white and white is the color of death. Boy! Talk about worry warts!

Fish - I cannot recall eating fish on the first of January but some people will eat fish and they tell me the fish represents silver money that will come to you throughout the coming year.

Desserts - People who have ring cake for dessert on the first day of the year will tell you the ring represents, "The Circle of Life," or "The Continuation of Life."

Naturally, the favorite dessert in the South for the beginning of a new year is peach pie or peach cobbler. There are several words that define the meaning of having peaches for the New Year. They range from humble, to health, to sweetness and to my favorite which has to be….. "Love!"

Since I probably will not have peaches for the first, I'm going to leave that third black-eyed pea on my plate. It's a CYA move in the romance category.

HAPPY NEW YEAR TO YOU! MAY IT ALWAYS BE PEACEFUL, HEALTHY, WEALTHY, SWEET AND ENDLESSLY ROMANTIC FOR ALL OF US!

Fat Tuesday in Athens

Mardi Gras in Athens - Fat Tuesday sneaked up on me in Athens. It's easy to sneak up on me these days because I'm not alert, quick and graceful as I once was. This is pretty much a lie because I have never been any of those things as I recall and certainly Katie Mae has never complimented me on having any of these attributes. To be truthful she says I am as alert and quick as a somnambulant snail and as graceful as a waltzing tortoise.

The importance of the moment hit me when I saw an ad in the Athens Banner-Herald that told me there is a "New Orleans 'N Athens" right downtown. And sure enough because of our love of acronyms, it is called "NONA."

I threw on my old "Fat Tuesday" togs and headed downtown. Katie Mae refused to go with me and I had a hard time driving because my "Cat Woman" mask kept slipping over my nose. When I parked I saw a blind pan handler with a seeing-eye dog. Since I couldn't see through the mask, I gave him twenty bucks to use the dog a little while. I headed inside NONA to catch the full force of all the Athens Mardi Gras action.

It was a disaster. The place was full of college kids. I asked the girl who met me at the door if she were a waitress. She informed me she was a barista. I don't speak Spanish. I thought she was telling me she was a bastard. I thought it strange that she should want to share with me that her parents were unmarried when she was conceived but you never know how crazy people get during Mardi Gras. Maybe all those beads were cutting off circulation to that miniscule brain of hers.

I think they were expecting a featured entertainer because she took a look at my gray hair and she asked me if I were "Fat Tuesday." I said, "Listen kid, I am not only fat on Tuesday but I am also fat the following Wednesday and right on up through the next Monday."

I asked for a drink and she carded me. They do that all the time in Athens. I'm obviously real old so I always think they are carding me to steal my identity and then it hits me that nobody in the world would want to be me. She took one look at my card and said, "You are not only Fat this Tuesday but you are too damned old to be in here!"

I attempted to angrily storm out of the joint but my big feet got caught up in a bar stool leg and the dog's leash lassoed me around the ankles. As I pitched face forward over a table full of fancy cocktails the dog got excited and bit me on the butt.

Having seen how effectively a seeing-eye dog can lacerate buttocks, none of the staff would come to my rescue. The dog, the staff and I were at a serious impasse. I could tell they didn't want me in there but they were afraid to touch me. I crawled out of there on my own. I was crawling and yelling bloody murder the whole way. The patrons gave me a wide berth. The dog had become docile but I couldn't help notice he was grinning at me.

When I got the dog back to his master, I told him the dog hadn't helped much and he said, "Yeah, I know. I just keep him around because I feel sorry for him. Hell, he can't see either. He has bitten me ten or twelve times in the last couple of years. You'd think the dumb barista would know me by now." It sounded like he was calling the dog a dumb bastard but I was in a state of wounded confusion. I have a hard time hearing when my buttocks have been lacerated.

The only thing I think I learned by going to Mardi Gras in Athens is don't try to be a young stud in a wild bar full of masked college kids. It is a futile pursuit and the experience will eventually leave you with the black ass.

Mardi Gras, The Real Deal - Mobile, AL, Not Athens, Georgia

I have to admit I embellished a bit (more like lied a lot) when I wrote about Mardi Gras at a downtown bar in Athens, Georgia but I have actually been to Mardi Gras functions in Mobile, Alabama. Mobile holds the claim to fame when it comes to the first Mardi Gras celebrations in the US.

Mobile began their Mardi Gras carnival celebrations in 1703. This was fifteen years before New Orleans was even thunk of.

Katie Mae and I lived in Mobile for a few months after we were wed back in 1974. She worked with a printing company whose owner was an old Mobilian and a member of one of the Mardi Gras secretive mystic societies. The mystic societies throw all the big dances and balls and organize the parades during Mardi Gras. I'm unsure of the name of his group of mystics. I think it was a secret.

His daughter who was a young sweet native of that wild and wicked old town took me and Katie Mae to her father's society ball. The girls were all dolled up in much finery and big bushy dresses and they smelled so sweet I kept swooning and falling down. Maybe I fell a lot because; I had a drink….. I had a couple of drinks….. I got drunk.

There was no doubt in my mind that I was looking good but I think the real reason I kept falling down was the rented tux coat was for a guy about the height of Shaquille O'Neal and it had tails and the black tie and a lovely neat white shirt with a hand full of funny little buttons that came with it. It even had fancy buttons for the cuffs which came in a separate box.

The tails kept dragging the floor. If you want to really understand the word "comeuppance," just wear a coat with long fish tails in a room full of older, heavy-set people. I finally had to sit out the dances which made Katie Mae (and me) much happier. It took me over a month to get over the whip-lashing.

Anyhow we made it through the ball and all that jerky dancing (for me) and on Fat Tuesday our wonderful little hostess took us into town to watch all those wild parade floats go by. The masked members of the mystic societies stand on the floats as they pass by and they grace the great unwashed commoners standing in the cluttered streets below with "Throws." Throws are colored beads, and Frisbees, and sweet cakes and faux gold doubloons and all kinds of other trinkets and sweets but most cherished of all the throws, I have learned, is............ MOON-PIES.

The first mistake made was mine. I saw a tiny old grandmotherly figure of a woman with a small boy who looked to be three or four years old. I decided I would give her a hand catching some trinkets and sweets thrown from the floats and then she could give them to the little lad. There were so many excited younger people thronging the streets you could see the reflection of colored beads and moon pies in their feverish eyes and I felt sure Granny was going to have a difficult time catching any of the throws for the little boy.

As soon as the first fist full of beads and moon pies hit the sidewalk, Granny knocked me on my ass. I never saw her again but I felt her run up my back and step on my head as she followed the float down the street. I thanked God that Granny was not a heavy woman and I had survived that severe stomping.

Things pretty much leveled out after that, parade wise, and as I watched the floats go by, I tried to push my back deep into the granite facade of the bank where we were standing so no more old women could find room to run up my back.

As the parade began to wind down our hostess grabbed us by the hands and we ran through a couple of alleys to a spot on a street corner where we could watch the parade's grand finale.

The grand finale consisted of these same masked men throwing more sweets and trinkets off the floats only this time I began to experience an odd feeling as if something frightful and sinister was afoot. Something told me to be careful. I think it was getting knocked on my ass by a 75 year old woman.

I was cautiously backing up a step or two when I realized the guys on the floats had an abundance of moon pies left over and they were picking them up by the box full to throw to the crowd. As I looked around I saw this crowd consisted of only small black children roiling like hungry minnows at the sides of the floats.

The guys on the floats began to dump box after box of moon pies into the thickening school of minnows at their feet. That harmless pool of small fishes instantly transformed into a shark-like feeding frenzy of little black kids trying to see who could grab the most moon pies. I was amazed and transfixed to the sidewalk as if I were paralyzed. Then to my utter astonishment we were stormed by the kids as one of the moon pie throwers unloaded a case of them right on top of Katie Mae's head. Katie Mae and our young friend were suddenly swept off their feet and they instantly began to disappear across a wave of backs of bent over little children grabbing and snatching for the moon pies on the asphalt. It looked as if the two girls were being swept away by rogue waves at the beach.

The Lord was still with me. At the last second I regained my senses long enough to shut my gaping mouth and reach out and grab each girl by a foot. I dragged them back across the undulating backs of all those moon-pie crazed children and when I got them back on their feet I hustled them as far from that crowd as fast as we could limp away.

The last thing I saw as I looked back was a lone girl about ten years old screaming and cursing and holding an empty moon pie box as high as she could hold it. If her curses could have exacted revenge on all those who made off with the contents of that box the city of Mobile would still be trying to identify the bodies of all those little boys who had literally trampled her to seize the booty. I was glad my Mother was not there to hear that rant. I still blush when I remember the things she screamed in outraged anger.

That's how we learned an old and cherished tradition of Mardi Gras in Mobile, Alabama. We were part of that tradition for only a few minutes but that is how I learned a most valuable lesson. Moon Pies can kill you and you don't even have to eat one.

If you are ever having a good time down on that part of the old Gulf Coast around Mardi Gras time, remember two things: Rip tides can be extremely dangerous. You might just happen to encounter a rip tide at the beach, however, some will occur when you least expect them. Always be aware of the scents in the air in Mobile, Alabama. Just the whiff of a moon pie crust can suddenly create a sidewalk rip tide of small children, driven like hunger-crazed sharks to the source of that sweet moon pie aroma!

My Funny (Belated) Valentine and Insane Tulips!

I know that Valentine's Day was the fourteenth of this month and I am sharing my strange story a couple of weeks after the fact but I am an old person and I get a senior's pass. I gave it to myself. You can do the same thing. Just give yourself a senior's pass anytime you want. You deserve it.

However, when it comes to buying a Valentine for your sweetheart you cannot get a senior's pass. You throw on some presentable rags and drag your ragged old fanny out there in the public world and you get that sweet other half (if you still have one and, if you do, be glad you do) a card that will make her smile as her heart jumps with joy. None of that probably works for you anymore but you can always dream on, especially around Valentine's Day. Blackmail of the direst sort occurs on Valentine's Day but don't let it get you down. Embrace it and love the one you're with!

It's Esther Howland's fault. She started making and selling the cards way back in the 1840's up in Massachusetts. Nowadays only Christmas cards outsell Valentine's Day cards. Over a million people make that inescapable trek to the store so they can help buy over 145 million Valentines for their loved ones. The Valentine's Day trio of compulsory purchases includes the card, the chocolates and the bouquet of roses. I have little will power but I am blessed with an unfaltering faith that the image I see in the mirror each morning is truly my own so I skip the chocolates.

The prediction for Valentine's chocolate sales this year (in real dollars) was one billion. That's with a "B" for those of you tracking the economy. Who knows how much is spent on flowers but statistics say 70% of all roses sold are red. Most women like softer hues but we are men and we cannot remember that women prefer lighter colors. We like red. Red is probably one of the few colors we can actually see. We are color blind most of the time. It is good to have women around to tell us when a color is something other than red.

Katie Mae and I shopped for Valentines together. We are not great lovers of cut roses. Katie Mae has taught me to prefer tulips. We were in Wal-Mart and we could find nothing but hundreds of bouquets of roses. Finally we found a pot of red tulips that were not yet in full bloom. We chose the plant. There were no cut tulips. Could we be the only weird couple in East Athens that loves tulips more than roses?

We went to the gift card section together. We went through about a hundred cards until we each found just the right card for the other. I turned to Katie Mae and I said, "If I were going to spend eight bucks for this Valentine, this is the one I would buy for you." Katie Mae picked out a very nice card and said, "If I were going to buy you a Valentine, I would buy this one for you." We told each other how much we liked the cards and loved the messages inside and that we loved each other and then we put the cards back on the shelf.

A guy standing next to us started laughing and said to me, "Now that woman really knows how to shop." I said, "Yes sir, she is a great shopper and a wonderful woman and we can't see spending almost twenty bucks on a couple of cards we'll never look at again!" He laughed again, put his card back on the rack and as he walked away, I heard him mumble, "I gotta go find my wife."

We took our fond memories of the purloined Valentine images and the tulips to the house. The tulips were on the little table in the kitchen area for less than a full week when we determined they were not mentally well. They drooped and the color had deepened to a dark dried-blood-like shade that cast a curious pall over the entire room. Katie Mae quickly banished the pot to the garage and sure enough, a couple of days later it had wilted down to an indescribable scrubby eyesore.

Valentine's Day in Athens was good for us. We exchanged unforgettable declarations of undying love right there amongst the gift card section at Wal-Mart, we saved money on cards we did not buy and we barely escaped the curse of a crazy red tulip.

Talking Dog in Athens, Georgia. Do Your Dogs Talk Back?

In Athens, Georgia - This weekend for thirty nine bucks you can see a fellow by the name of Tod Oliver perform with his dog Irving, who is billed as "Irving the Talking Dog." Tod and Irving will be on stage at the UGA's Ramsey Concert Hall. If you are a dog lover, I know you will want to go see Tod and Irving.

By the way, Tod Oliver is a ventriloquist and there might be some trickery involved in Irving's vocalizing. If you go see Tod, you can be the judge of whether old Irving can speak for himself or not.

Now the article I read was written by Karah-Leigh Hancock in The Athens Banner Herald. I don't know Karah-Leigh Hancock but I suspect a woman with a hyphenated name probably has a dog and she probably talks to her dog. I'll bet Karah-Leigh is no kin to my old friend Rose Hancock because Rose and I come from a generation and a kind that does very little talking to dogs unless, of course, they are Georgia Bulldawgs and they can really talk back. Take it from me, I have never met a Georgia Bulldawg who could not talk back, and with great volume too.

Kareh-Leigh raises my level of suspicion about her style of reporting and Tod Oliver's true ambition in life from the get-go. She says, right off, "Did you ever wonder what goes on inside a dog's head?" My answer would have to be, right off, "not ever!"

She quotes Tod Oliver as saying, "I didn't care about getting paid. I cared about making a good living." Now, she either misquoted that boy or his thoughts along the lines of, "where is my next meal coming from," are so convoluted that I can only believe he has not really been talking to Irving the Talking Dog. If Tod Oliver did not care about getting paid then he, no doubt, should have checked with Irving. Maybe that's how Tod found out that Irving can talk. Irving heard Tod say, "I didn't care about getting paid." It was at that moment Irving took Tod's ankle in his mouth and took him around the corner to have a private chat with him. It was then that Irving first spoke to Tod and told him, "I don't know how you really feel about getting paid but the first time I start to drool because you are tardy with the food, you can kiss my dog ass goodbye!"

So Irving taught Tod how to understand "getting paid," and "making a living" are synonymous. It has worked well because neither of them looked anorexic in their picture in the Athens newspaper.

You be the judge. Do you really need to pay to see a guy who has a dog that actually talks to him or do you believe, with great faith, (as I do) that dog lovers are always talking to their dogs and they always hear the dog reply?

That's my excellent reason for saving the thirty nine bucks. All my dog-owning, dog-loving friends speak to their dogs. I am convinced dog owners can hear their pets replying to them. I often hear the loving owner repeat what the dog has said and it makes perfect sense. I don't think I need to hear Irving the Talking Dog's voice. I know dogs can talk. I think it is wonderful that so many people have brilliant, intelligent, and wise four-legged friends who can easily console their owners without vocalizing or using sign language. ESP works just fine between owner and pet and if it works for them, it works for me.

I do draw the line at kissing the dog or in any way allowing the dog to kiss me or lick me on the lips. Dogs have absolutely no modesty and shame when it comes to licking their own bottoms. They even lick the bottoms of dogs they don't know and to whom they have never been properly introduced. While most owners consider a kiss or lick on the mouth from their dog to be a loving kiss, I suspect most dogs do not really love you that intensely and they are giving you an acrimonious taste of malice and spite.

If you insist on kissing the dog, be sure your dog really loves you and never, never French kiss the dog.

II - THE KENSLEY REPORTS

Kensley is our dear, sweet Grand Niece. For a number of years now she has come to visit us for two weeks in the summer. Kensley and Katie Mae refer to this annual summer visit as, "Camp Kay." We plan a number of projects we can tackle with Kensley's help and guidance. I especially need the guidance. Over the years we have made soap, jewelry, flutes from bamboo, and whatever else we think will be fun and entertaining. One year Kensley even learned the fundamentals of sewing and each summer she strives to create gifts for the less fortunate friends and relatives who do not get to come to "Camp Kay." When she is with us, her presence brightens our days and helps us stay young.

The Kensley Reports are daily e-mails to Kensley's mother to keep her informed of our progress on our projects. As you can tell from the reports, Kensley has a vivid and sometimes startling imagination. These reports are from July, 2012.

The Kensley Report #1 – 2012

The Kensley Report-I - Came into Statesboro Thursday July 5. Cason rode with us. He talks a lot and he wanted to ride shotgun but we put him in the back seat and duct taped the little movie screen to his big head. Aunt Kay had ribs and potatoes and peas and rolls and corn on the cob and a birthday cake. I ate three pounds of cherry tomatoes. Uncle Ben only has four tomato plants this year but he says Wal-Mart has stacks of tomatoes on shelves and in coolers in town and not to worry about a tomato shortage. He also has a map to Strickland Farms where we can haul 55 gallon drums and pick our own tomatoes. Tomorrow we are going to a computer store where we can get a calculator with more than twelve digits so we can calculate how many drums of tomatoes we will need for my two week visit. Did I mention how much I like tomatoes?

Things were pretty quiet last night (that's not really true because Cason was here). Uncle Ben does not call him Cason. He calls him "Rambling Red Roberts. He says the rambling does not mean Cason wanders about. It means Cason's mouth has been clocked at 83 miles per hour on a zig-zag course. Uncle Ben says Cason can ask you six questions, answer two of them himself, forget three of them and tell you he really didn't want to know the answer to the last one, all in the space of 49 seconds. He said Cason could stay here too and we would let him swim in the little pond out back every morning but Cason backed out when he learned he was going to have to get out of a burlap bag I'll put him in before we toss him in the pond.

Tomorrow we crank up the "jewry" business again. I think we're calling the new production company, Kreations by Ken Ken.

The Kensley Report #2 – 2012

The Kensley Report–II – Sorry about yesterday's report. We got busy plotting the expected success of the jewry manufacturing business. I had Uncle Ben helping me with a special spring hook that goes on earrings. He sneezed and clapped his hand over his mouth. The ring got hooked in his nose. I wanted to take him to the emergency room but Aunt Kay said she could use him like that and to just leave the ring in his nose. We went next door to the Harvey's house to celebrate the sale of our house. Mrs. Harvey had pigs-in-a-blanket. I ate 14 of them. I just ate the bread. Uncle Ben ate the little pieces of sausage. He wanted me to eat 10 or 12 more so he could have enough sausage to make a hot dog. Mrs. Harvey gave us funny looks. Aunt Kay made us get up and go home. They live right next door so Uncle Ben thought it would be okay if I drove us over. Aunt Kay's car was still smoking this morning. I don't think the pine tree is going to make it. Those air bags really do a good job. I didn't lose a single tooth.

My site on "Etsy" is named "KreationsbyKenKen. When we named it the stupid thing wouldn't let us put spaces between the words. Production of the jewry went well but Uncle Ben had a tough time taking pictures of it. First he tried with his iphone and then he used my phone and then Aunt Kay's ipad and finally he tried Aunt Kay's camera. He had a horrible time getting the pictures to look good and getting them on the website. He said it would be easier if he weren't so computer crazed. He also said a lot of other things I couldn't understand. I asked Aunt Kay and she said not to worry because Uncle Ben speaks a strange language and often curses in more than one tongue. Can you tell me the meaning of "jammersluck?" Anyhow that's what it sounded like when he got the ring stuck in his nose and later when he was stomping that camera into little pieces.

The Kensley Report #3 – 2012

The Kensley Report- III –Today we left Uncle Ben still mumbling some of those strange words and working on the "Etsy" project while we went to see a Katy Perry movie. I wanted to see Magic Mike and I tried to get Aunt Kay to slip down the entrance hallway a door or two so we could catch old Mike in action. She said she would like to see that movie but she didn't want to have to leave me chained by myself in a chair watching Katy Perry while she had all the fun. We went and bought groceries. Aunt Kay said she hurt her back putting the bottled water in the trunk. Uncle Ben said, "Why didn't you let old slim here help you?" He meant me. Aunt Kay said, "As soon as I got the car started, Ken Ken sat down in the cool air. She can't stand to grocery shop." Uncle Ben said, "You don't help your Momma with the groceries?" I said, "I don't go to the grocery store with my Mother." Uncle Ben said, "What in the world are you going to do when you're out on your own?" I said, "My husband is going to buy my groceries and carry them for me." Uncle Ben got choked on a chicken leg and when we managed to get the purple out of his face he gasped, "I always knew you were going to be the perfect Lady Bulldawg!"

We are revisiting past projects. Uncle Ben likes saving soap and boiling it in huge pots and then pouring it into molds shaped like gerbils. We did soap a few years ago so we are looking for another project. He said he used to scrape the Mennen's Speed Stick remnants from the plastic containers, melt them down and pour them back into the containers. He said he always thought it worked great for him until one night he and Aunt Kay went to a nice party and he was left standing alone on the dance floor when everyone there cleared the room. Even the band left but not before the drummer tried to beat him to death with a tambourine. He said it was hard to believe that a little hint of BO would clear a room like that!

The Kensley Report #4 – 2012

The Kensley Report IV– Today was a strange day. I almost had to force myself to sleep until noon. It was tough but I made it. A nurse came to see Uncle Ben. She even weighed him with scales she had in her car. Uncle Ben told her that scales hauled around in a car are never accurate and her scales were busted. She told him he was fat. She asked him a lot of questions about his health habits and I don't think he told her the truth the whole time. She kept giving him strange looks and when I later asked him why, he said, "I told her that one of my eyes is green and the other one is blue but you really can't see it except in a certain light so she was just trying to catch me in the right light." Aunt Kay said, "Uncle Ben lies. I saw him winking at that nurse."

He did tell her how bright and kreative I am and that I was making jewelry for sell on Etsy. The nurse bought a bracelet and earrings from me. She was out of cash and blank checks so we let her take the goods and gave her a stamped self-addressed envelope so she can mail Aunt Kay the funds and Aunt Kay has already paid me the cashola. Uncle Ben says you must never forget to sell and don't be shy about talking about the money right up front. He says if the nurse doesn't send him the money for the jewelry that he'll call her company and tell them she called him fat and, in spite of that, the whole time she was calling him fat she insisted on winking at him.

We went to see their realtor. He said I remind him of his daughter who is twelve and goes to Bulloch Academy. He left the room and Uncle Ben says that no way is his daughter cuter than I am because Bulloch Academy girls aren't as cute as Deerfield girls.

We went to a Mexican Restaurant that looks like an East Indian cat house according to Uncle Ben. Uncle Ben and I had cokes. Aunt Kay had seven frozen margaritas. Uncle Ben said coke makes him dizzy so I had to drive home. Uncle Ben sat me on the spare tire and taped the tire iron to my right leg so I could reach the gas pedal. He said not to worry about the brakes. He would teach me how they used to play "no brakes" when he was in high school. It all worked out fine. Aunt Kay had dozed off and did not notice when I had to go into a ditch to pass a big cement truck that stopped suddenly in front of us.

Tomorrow I volunteer at the hospital gift shop with Aunt Kay. I'm really excited. I get to eat free. I hope they have plenty of cherry tomatoes in the cafeteria.

The Kensley Report #5 – 2012

The Kensley Report- V –Today was a great day for me as one of America's indefatigable volunteers. Aunt Kay and I took the gift shop at East Georgia Regional hospital by storm. We had the keyboard on the cash register so hot they had to call in a triage team to water it down. Uncle Ben had warned me about eating all the candy in the shop so I just concentrated on the job at hand and waited until lunch time before I cleaned the cafeteria out of fried chicken and Dr. Pepper. I had on my sharp new khaki long legged britches, a red youth volunteer knit shirt (they gave me, I think) and an official badge (they gave me, I know, because it has my picture on it) to show folks I was an old hand at this and on top of things.

We had to stock the cooler with a shipment of flowers that came in and I got my head stuck in the sliding glass door but Aunt Kay was quick and she put her foot up on the cooler for leverage and snatched me out by my legs. My head got scratched up a little bit, my hair was all tangled and I still have a couple of pounds of pollen up my nose but I'm okay.

Aunt Kay had told me that sometimes strange people come in the gift shop and share weird stories about their lives with her and often they tell her a lot more than she wants to know. She wanted to be sure I didn't get scared so I was pretty cool for a while but it did shock me more than a little bit when an old woman came in. She said she had a collie with fourteen puppies and the mama dog didn't have but 13 teats. I didn't know what to say so I just eased around the counter and high-tailed it to the back room. Aunt Kay sold her 14 Auburn binkies for the puppies. Aunt Kay gave the woman a discount on the binkies in hopes the woman would hurry up and leave.

Later when I told Uncle Ben about her, he said "Any damned fool knows a dog doesn't have that many nipples and if she's so dumb she can't count past twelve she should be breeding goats."

The Kensley Report #6 – 2012

The Kensley Report-VI –We've had to put our latest projects under top-secret wraps. Uncle Ben says if our plans are revealed, the Chinese will be on our doorstep in the morning and they will kidnap us and whisk us away to some God-forsaken place in Outer Mongolia and we'll be imprisoned in a sweat-box of a work shop and forced to produce copies of our latest invention. He says they steal our American ideas then they produce products created from our ideas to sell back to us in order to eventually own us body and soul. He put black-out curtains on all the windows and had us whispering in the dark. He also made Aunt Kay fry the pork chops under a beach towel so their eavesdropping devices would be confused by the muffled sizzling. Just in case we're captured he made me practice eating fried okra with chop sticks.

Our secret plans went temporarily awry when we were in Wally World waiting in line in one of their most popular departments. There was a big country guy in front of us who, despite his large size, had lost his butt somewhere. It looked like a family with six children had moved out of the seat of his pants. Naturally this resulted in our being subjected to an unobstructed view of his bare behind every time he leaned forward. Uncle Ben said, "Quick, quick, get your camera out. YouTube is paying small fortunes for shots of Wal-Mart people with plumber's butt." I started laughing and couldn't get my camera so Uncle Ben got his camera and was snapping away and then he messaged the YouTube folks to see how much they were paying for pictures of oversized farm boys showing a good five inches of gaping buttocks. He was really disappointed when they sent back a note that there were over three million people on YouTube trying to sell similar snapshots taken in Wal-Mart. You should have seen his face fall. I started laughing even harder. The big man turned around with a big snarl and said, "What's so funny?"

Uncle Ben looked up at him and said, "Don't worry. She'll be okay. She gets silly and giddy every time she eats fried okra with chop sticks."

Tomorrow the people who want to buy the house are sending over a nit-picker (according to Uncle Ben) to inspect the house. Uncle Ben says the guy might become aggravating. If he does, Uncle Ben says he will run over the guy with his riding mower to distract him a little bit. He thinks the ambulance and the EMT's trying to put the guy's leg back on him will be a pretty good distraction.

The Kensley Report #7 - 2012

The Kensley Report-VII - Today we had the nit-picker come by but he was a pretty cool guy so Uncle Ben didn't have to run him over with the lawn mower. Besides he was young and big and strong so Uncle Ben told me he would give the guy a pass on having to rough him up a bit. Aunt Kay and I went to get her hair cut and Uncle Ben said before the guy left he told Uncle Ben that he had two loose shingles. I think Uncle Ben was mad. I heard him mumbling something about, "You don't just walk into a stranger's house and start telling him he's got loose shingles. That's just rude! I started to tell him I may have two loose shingles but you are ugly as hell and I can get those shingles fixed tomorrow but you'll still be ugly!" Then the guy told Uncle Ben that he also was a roofer. Uncle Ben said, "I'll bet that guy finds loose shingles on every house he inspects. I should have run over him with the lawn mower." There was an empty beautician's chair at the salon so I got in it and spun around, and spun around and spun around and then stood up and then fell over and hit my mouth on the sink they wash hair in and broke the enamel off the sink. My teeth don't look too bad. Aunt Kay and Miss Charlene wired them back in using some haywire and old rusty pliers Miss Charlene found in her husband's tackle box in a car he abandoned in the back parking lot in 1957. Aunt Kay said it's a good thing Miss Anna can work miracles with crooked and cracked teeth.

We met Uncle Ben at Moe's for lunch. Uncle Ben had never eaten at a Moe's before. He said it's very likely he will never eat at Moe's again. He says after over 60 years of a misspent youth, his stomach does better on apple sauce and Gerber baby foods. He kept asking the staff if they had ever heard Louis Jordan sing, "Five Guys Named Moe." None of them had heard of the song but Uncle Ben persisted. He asked each person about three or four times. Then Aunt Kay and I had to listen to him name about a thousand things named Moe. He started off with Little Moe and Big Moe and Four-Eyed Moe and Cross-Eyed Moe and he went on to No Moe and Plenty Moe. Then he came to short Moe and Tall Moe and when he ran out of guys named Moe he started in on Moe descriptions like Moe Bettah and Moe Worser. He went on into Mogrits Moe and Motea Moe and finally Aunt Kay stared him down with a fierce glare and said, "No mo Moe or I will strangle you in slow mo." He finally shut up. We left carrying a big bag of heartburn. I think Moe's staff will be really happy if Uncle Ben never eats there again.

The battery in Aunt Kay's remote control key for her Toyota died. She told Uncle Ben that her user's manual said to be very careful when handling the battery. Uncle Ben said, "That's just Toyota's way of gypping you out of your money. I'll bet they charge you forty bucks to put a new battery in that remote control!" So he went to five places trying to find the right battery for the control. He finally found one for $6.41 at Radio Shack and he gleefully bragged to me that he found one for $6.41 and probably saved about $35.00 by not getting one from Toyota. When he got home, he even called Toyota and asked them how much they charged for the battery. The guy told him, "Four bucks. "Uncle Ben said, "What??" The guy said, "Four bucks!" Uncle Ben said, "How much do you charge for installing it in the remote control?" The guy said, "Nothing, we just open it up and pop it in for free." Uncle Ben has not mentioned the battery any more.

We think Etsy is a big flop for us. We spent hours trying to get the photos of the jewelry bright and clear and they turned out looking like slides of anemic amoebae from the Center for Disease Control. The pictures are about the size of postage stamps and you can't really tell what's in the pictures. Apparently you cannot enlarge them. It took so long to finally get them on the website because every time Uncle Ben would confirm his e-mail address, Etsy would send another message asking him to confirm his e-mail address. Uncle Ben says the people who designed the website are not mentally well and if he could arrange a meeting with them and break some kneecaps, we could cure their mental problems and probably get better results but then he just shook his head and said, "Probably not." He says he's going to buy me one of those suitcases that folds out into a display and has legs on it so I can sell my jewelry on street corners in big cities and for my protection he's going to send a trained gorilla (not a jungle warfare fighter but a very large monkey) with a machete and a box of hand grenades with me.

The Kensley Report #8 – 2012

The Kensley Report VIII– Today was only a half-lazy day. I actually beat the sun before it got twelve o'clock high by two hours. Uncle Ben went outside and worked in the yard. Aunt Kay always checks on him because he walks funny and sometimes walks into trees or falls down. We watched him through a window as he pruned a couple of trees. He kept leaping into the air and cutting off limbs with his lopper. We were amazed. Sometimes he would reach a height of five or six inches. When he finally came back in we asked him why he was jumping up and lopping limbs and he said he was too lazy to go get a ladder. He looked a little pained and I heard him tell Aunt Kay he thinks he further fractured several vertebrae. Now he walks even funnier and falls down more.

I curled Aunt Kay's hair. I put an upward and outward curl on her hair and Uncle Ben said her hair looks like the hat on The Flying Nun or she looks like a middle-aged Pippi Longstocking with dark hair and her pigtails half gone. Aunt Kay gave Uncle Ben one of those "Now or later" looks, meaning, "You'll shut up now if you want something to eat and a place to sleep later."

Aunt Kay made vegetable soup and used a hambone for seasoning. She fried cornbread just like Daddy loves and I would have eaten my seventeenth piece but Uncle Ben was reaching for it too and he still has pretty good strength in his left hand and I thought I was going to lose my right arm at the shoulder if I didn't pull it back pretty quick. He's fast for an old man when he gets greedy.

He asked me if I had ever heard the "Hambone" and when I said no, he stood up from the table and started slapping his leg back and forth with his hand and yelling, "Hambone, Hambone have you heard, Papa's gone buy me a mocking bird? And if dat mocking bird don't sing Papa's gone buy me a diamond ring." At the end of each line he would pop his lips with his hand and it sounded like a cork popping out of a wine bottle. I think there were more verses to the "Hambone" but I saw Aunt Kay picking up his plate with the cornbread from the table so he immediately shut up and sat back down. I don't know if he feared missing the rest of his supper or it could have been the damage he was doing to his lips that made him sit down. They had turned that dark purple bruised look.

He said when he was about ten or eleven he would watch football practice at Hugh Mills Memorial Stadium and small black boys would do the "Hambone" for the varsity high school football players. The players would pay the boys for performing. They would get a couple of nickels or sometimes even a quarter but they would not do the "Hambone" for Don Braswell because one time instead of paying them, Don took his glass eye out of its socket and chased them all over the field. Uncle Ben said his brother Billy who played on the team with Don said that sometimes they would have to stop football practice, and even one time they had to stop a regulation football game, so everybody could search for Don's eye when it popped out after he took a good lick. Uncle Ben waited until I had finished my soup and cornbread before he told me the story about the glass eye.

He told me Billy dated a beautiful girl named Lillian Lackland. He said a man told him not long ago that he worked for a fellow who owned a hardware store who used to walk around in the store saying. "Silly Lilly loves Billy Swilley." Lillian's mother used to come around to the grammar schools to teach them how to speak clearly and correctly. He said everybody loved her but it must have been impossible for her to get the redneck out of them. She would finish at their school and move on to the next school but they all continued to speak with such a Southern drawl even kids with ADHD would fall asleep in about two minutes.

He says we didn't have ADHD in Albany before all those little Yankee military brats came to town with their Air Force and Marine dads. The poor local kids who drawled a lot never got a word in edgewise until they learned to talk fast like the Yankee kids. Uncle Ben says all that fast talking made the poor local kids really nervous and they began to develop ADHD from talking faster than their oral development would allow.

He said he loved Mrs. Lackland but he couldn't say the same for Mrs. Perry. She was a music director for the school system. She came around to Broad Avenue School one morning and had each first grader stand by her piano and sing out a note she struck on the piano. When it was Uncle Ben's turn he said he sang so beautifully canaries would have killed for a note like that but Mrs. Perry stifled a belly laugh, looked sadly at his teacher, Mrs. Brim, and slowly shook her head. Uncle Ben says that was crushing to him. It happened almost 65 years ago and his feelings are still hurt. I think the grudge he harbors in his heart is easily aroused whenever Miss Perry's name is mentioned.

Tomorrow if we get up before noon, Uncle Ben says we need to go to auctions or antique stores or regular old yard sales and test my youthful ability to use ESP to identify valuable objects we might buy for pennies and then sell for great fortunes on E-Bay or Amazon. He's had me practicing on handling objects and relating any flashes of precognitive details that might occur to me. I think that's a great idea but I think he should have started out with something more interesting than a pair of his old socks covered in a plastic shopping bag from Wal-Mart.

The Kensley Report #9 – 2012

The Kensley Report-IX – I think today was a repeat of yesterday. I woke up about ten o'clock and Uncle Ben put me to work recovering pictures and documents he has secreted in all kinds of weird places on his computer. He doesn't understand how to name files. He says that for many years when he was working, folders always went into files and now, on computers, the files go into folders. He says computer geeks do things like that to give old people anxiety attacks. He has some files with names like Dragonseed which was a book he read when he was about ten. He has no idea what is in the file or why he named it that or why he saved it. He has about ten folders named, "Kay's Camera." He says that's easy to remember and if someone wants a copy of a picture, he says, "Look on my computer under "Kay's Camera." He says that keeps nosy people busy for a while. He has no memory of any password, ever. He says nobody can rip off his password because he has to use a new one every time he goes onto a protected website.

We talked about favorite colors. Mine is blue. Aunt Kay and Uncle Ben favor green. Uncle Ben says that over 40% of people in many of the countries in the world like the color blue best. He said he cannot remember when he did not use a green toothbrush. When I asked why he said one of the first things he notices in the mornings is the toothbrush in his hand and he loves the color green so a green toothbrush makes him happy in the mornings. He said the only time a green toothbrush failed to make him happy was when Paul played soccer and he was with Aunt Kay and a bunch of soccer parents in a motel in Macon. Uncle Ben had bought a new green electric toothbrush. While brushing his teeth that next morning, he fell asleep at the lavatory. The toothbrush jumped out of his mouth, loosened a tooth, ripped his lip, left a furrow across his cheek and wound up scratching his right ear lobe. When he finally got himself straightened out and in the lobby with Aunt Kay and the other soccer parents, Aunt Kay leaned over and whispered, "You've got soap in your ear." Uncle Ben said, "That's not soap." Aunt Kay said, "Then what is it?" Uncle Ben said, "It's toothpaste." Aunt Kay told me this story and she said she didn't say another word to him. She left the room for a while because she was determined that she was not going to ask him how he got toothpaste in his ear in front of all those people. She was afraid to hear the answer.

Uncle Ben worked in the yard today. One time I saw him pushing a small mower and it was hard to tell if he was pushing it or using it to keep from falling down. I never saw anybody use a lawnmower as a crutch before. He was going to grill some burgers but we couldn't get him to turn loose of the mower so Aunt Kay grilled them inside on a little George Foreman grill. Uncle Ben said George Foremen has eight sons and they are all named George. He says George Foreman either lacks imagination, or has an extremely short memory or is really lazy. He says we can't mention any of this to Mr. Foreman because he is a very large man who can drive your entire head deep into your chest cavity by just patting it.

Uncle Ben says names are really important and people should take care when naming pets and children. For example, he said, Uncle Geoffrey Gray had a dog he named "No No." Paul wanted to know how you disciplined a dog named No No. Paul had a good point. When No No was sent to obedience school, every time the trainers would try to stop one of No No's bad habits she thought they were calling her to lunch. That's right, No No was a girl. No No was kicked out of obedience school. The trainers said she had insurmountable psychological problems. Uncle Ben says that is my lesson for the day. "Watch what you name pets and children!"

The Kensley Report #10 – 2012

The Kensley Report-X –I almost beat Uncle Ben out of bed this morning. He did not get up until eleven o'clock and I slept past noon. Actually he said he got up about 4:00 AM and did a wild goat dance beneath the pine trees in the cul-de-sac in front of the house. According to him it's sort of a celebration of life for real old guys but it took its toll on his ability to remain awake past six o'clock so he went back to bed to replenish his energy. He talks funny sometimes. He says he usually only does the wild goat dance on a Friday night during a full moon but something inspired him to dance early this morning. He said a voice told him to dance. I told him that was probably a stray thought and you don't have to act on every stray thought you have. He said, "Oh." Apparently he has never had a real thought before.

I watched "Storage Hunters" all day. It was hour after hour of "Storage Hunters." Uncle Ben said, "I can't believe you're watching that rubbish. It's all mindless junk and is greatly responsible for the dumbing down of America." He said none of the so-called reality shows are real and every little crisis is staged for idiots with a ten second attention span so they won't switch channels. So I said, "Okay Uncle Ben, lets watch "Victorious" or "Good Time Charlie's" and Uncle Ben looked stunned for a minute and then said, "Nah, lets watch a couple of more hours of "Storage Hunters. I've got about five or six brain cells left and I need to salvage something out of this deal."

We ate at The Olive Garden. Aunt Kay said, "Look, I've got a coupon worth ten bucks at the Olive Garden!" Uncle Ben says, "Well, why don't we go there for dinner?" Then he says, "You know this is quite a challenge for me and Kensley and you are really putting us to the test because I'm sort of quasi-retired and Kensley is out of school for the summer and we don't take lightly to having to just up and take a bath and clean up all of a sudden for nothing more than going downtown in Statesboro, Georgia. Besides, I've got three layers of dirt on my feet that have kept them warm since Wednesday and Kensley took a bath just last Tuesday."

Aunt Kay said we were bathing and we were not going to talk about it anymore. Uncle Ben left the room because, as he says, since he has gotten older and he is not too sure that he can whip her in a fair fight anymore, he has chosen to become more obedient. He cleans up pretty well. Aunt Kay cut his hair and shined up the bald spots on his head until it looked as bright as a 1953 Hudson Hornet hubcap. I was going to watch her cut his hair but he had to remind us that he likes to get his hair cut while wearing a pair of old briefs and it would not be proper for me to stand around gawking at him in his unmentionables (whatever that means) and besides, he says, "This ain't no spectator sport."

When we got seated at The Olive Garden, Uncle Ben discovered a dead fly on our table. He said he was going to handle the problem discretely but when he brushed the fly away with his napkin, the fly stuck to the napkin and since it was a cloth napkin, I could see he was becoming a bit annoyed. He tried to control himself but when the hostess came over he said in a pretty good sized voice, "I'm not sure I can eat at the same table where this poor fly just fell over dead. You know, I think the fly was here first and it would be the right thing for us to do if y'all just gave us another table and that would give you time to properly dispose of his poor little body." The girl looked really embarrassed and after they moved us way back to a table right next to the restroom I noticed our service became much smoother and quicker. I could see people poking their heads from inside the waitress' station to take a look at us. I think they were hoping it wouldn't take us long to eat.

I said, "Uncle Ben you were pretty hard on her weren't you?" He said, "Not nearly as hard as I was on that gal in the new restaurant out on the Dawson Road who brought me an empty soup bowl to the table so I could get some soup from the buffet line and then she said, "Can I get you anything else?" I said to her, "Yes Ma'am, you can bring me another soup bowl and, this time, don't put your thumb in it. Ken Ken, sometimes if it ain't right you have to tell 'em. I know you and I are not put here on this earth to educate every dumb jackass that comes down the pike but sometimes you have to let them know they are wrong.

Unfortunately, it took us a pretty good while to eat. I could see the wait staff was getting more and more nervous because Uncle Ben takes naps at odd times and his head kept bobbing over and bouncing off the table from time to time and I was praying he would not get his face stuck in his seafood brodette bowl. Finally Aunt Kay and I finished up by dividing a Triple Chocolate Strata dessert and Uncle Ben paid the tab. I could hear him muttering, "My gosh, how in the world can two little short women like that eat that much doggoned food?" As we were about to leave, Aunt Kay exclaims "Oh no, I didn't use my ten dollar coupon!" Then we had to sit there on that bench near the cash register while the manager, the hostess, the waiter and two dishwashers tried to figure how to give us back our ten dollars. Uncle Ben began to make strange noises from somewhere deep in his body and I saw the waiter jerk his head in our direction and I could tell he was very alarmed because his eyes were getting bigger than the brodette bowls. He ran over to us and snatched a ten dollar bill out of his pocket, and said, "This ain't going to be hard to figure out because you paid us in cash so just take this ten dollar bill and we won't be holding y'all up any further.

Uncle Ben took the ten said, "Thank you my man," and we walked right out the front door as Uncle Ben explained to me again, "Sometimes you just gotta let 'em know if things ain't right.

The Kensley Report #11 - 2012

The Kensley Report-XI –Today was a great day for volunteering. I worked five hours helping Miss Christina, the gift shop manager, mark down the prices on lots of merchandise and doing an inventory of some of the items. They are going to reduce the inventory and some of the price mark-downs I did were as much as 75% off the original price. I heard the ladies in the gift shop mention the inventory needed to be reduced, so to help them out more, I went ahead and marked down everything I could get my hands on. Miss Christina is going to be so happy and proud of me for helping her to empty the place.

Uncle Ben said he could have helped by going around the hospital and giving the stuffed animals and teddy bears to the nurses. Aunt Kay said we were being too helpful and maybe it would be a good idea if I didn't mention to Miss Christina that I got carried away marking everything down.

They have Jim Shore and Willow Tree merchandise in the shop. Uncle Ben wanted to know what Willow Tree manufactured and Aunt Kay and I told him they make lovely little figurines of angels and people in different situations and the figurines had no faces. He said it was bad luck to make little statues with no faces. He said," I just don't get a true sense of fulfillment if the thing has no face. It reminds me of when I was in high school and I never could get a date. The girls I asked to go out would always give me blank looks." He also said there is no way to tell if a figurine is lovely if it has no face. "The little gal statuette might have a pretty good figure but she could look like a walrus in the face."

Aunt Kay and Uncle Ben left me in the gift shop and went grocery shopping. He hates it because he says most men can walk right in, buy what they want and go on home but a woman has to read every word on every label of every item she sees. He asked Aunt Kay if the wording had changed on any of those labels since last week and if it had he would speak to the manager about it if that would help speed up the grocery shopping process.

She said he is a real pain to go shopping with. He talks to everybody about any subject in the world. He saw a woman on her knees today trying to get a can off the bottom shelf and when she finally managed to stand up again he complimented her on her ability to get vertical without screaming. He said, "That was great. I would still be down there tomorrow if I had to do that. I did hear your knees and hips popping a little bit but you made it!" Aunt Kay said the woman gave him a very cold smile.

Uncle Ben loves the little white dog in the Travelers Insurance TV commercials and he will start singing "Trouble" in the aisles of the grocery store. He sings really loud if he is in an aisle by himself and when he rounds the corner into another aisle with people in it, he acts as if nothing has happened and he was not the person making that racket. Aunt Kay tries to control him but he will sometimes stand at the end of one aisle and yell to her, "Kay! You want some more of that Tube Rose snuff this week? You're about out of it." Now his dog is in another commercial and the dog has got Uncle Ben walking around singing to Aunt Kay, "Oh, I've been good, I've been good, I've been good to you!"

Tomorrow, Aunt Kay and I work our regular shift in the gift shop and I get to see Aunt Kay's Statesboro mothers, Miss Edith and Miss Moena. They volunteer at the front desk and they are very active. I say that because Miss Edith is 89 and Miss Moena is 90. Although they have a little age on them Uncle Ben doesn't cut them any slack. Sometimes after our morning shift ends and we are all walking to the cafeteria, Uncle Ben, will say, "You girls are going to have to pick up the pace a little, I have to be home by Thursday," or he'll say, "You ladies need to slow down a bit before I have to get the fire hose out to keep y'all from burning up this floor."

The Kensley Report #12 - 2012

The Kensley Report XII– Today I worked our regular shift in the gift shop at East Georgia Regional Hospital with Aunt Kay. Aunt Kay's Statesboro mothers, Miss Edith and Miss Moena, worked the information desk this morning too. They are right around the corner from the gift shop. The gift shop has a display case located in the Women's Pavilion that is used for displaying baby clothes (because that's where the babies are born). I mean in the Women's Pavilion, not the display case. Anyhow Aunt Kay and I took some sale signs down there to put on the display case and as we were passing this one door, Aunt Kay pointed to the sign on the door and said, "Do you know what that means?" I looked at the sign that read, "Morgue," and I answered, "No Ma'am," and she said, "That's where they keep the dearly departed." It took me a minute to figure out what she meant but it took her about two or three minutes to catch up with me after I understood. I could hear her footsteps running behind me and I could hear her gasping, "Slow down, slow down, they won't hurt you!"

We ate in the cafeteria. Miss Edith said she wasn't sure she wanted to walk down there with Uncle Ben because he made fun of how slow they walked. She said Miss Moena was the one slowing everybody down because she recently broke her hip and now she uses a cane with all kinds of psychedelic colors on it and when she looks down at her cane, she gets dizzy. Then we have to stop for a minute until Miss Moena's head clears.

I was in line with Mr. Darell who is the head of the volunteer services and Uncle Ben. When they served my plate, I got rice and spaghetti and Mr. Darell kept staring at my plate and he said, "Kensley, you're not going to get the meat sauce that goes on the spaghetti?" and Uncle Ben said, "Kensley is a weird eater. She is a carboholic. She eats rice and potatoes and pasta and white bread on wheat bread. Last night she ate five super-sized scoops of chocolate ice cream with about four ounces of chocolate syrup poured all over it and a half cup of chocolate chip morsels sprinkled all around. It took me a while to find a bowl big enough to hold it all." We talked about buying groceries because Aunt Kay and Uncle Ben usually buy groceries after Tuesday lunch in the hospital. They see Miss Edith in the grocery store a lot of times and she always looks at their shopping cart and shakes her head and says, "You have entirely too much food in that buggy!" Sometimes they will run when they see her because they know she will scold them for being such pigs.

Uncle Ben regretted bringing up the subject of women reading all the labels on the products in the grocery store because he thought Mr. Darell was going to back him up. Mr. Darell said, "I can't help you with that argument because I'm the one in my family who reads all the labels." He does a lot of the cooking in his house. So then Uncle Ben had to back track by saying "I guess that's right. Today's woman does not cook." Then I said, "You're right about that. I've got an aunt who has lived in her house for six years and she has never used her stove." Aunt Kay said, "Shhhhh, don't be telling all your family secrets."

Uncle Ben once asked Miss Moena about her name because it is unusual. It's pronounced "Mo-wee-na." She said she was named for a famous Georgian named Moina Michael but when her mother named her, she spelled it with an "e" instead of an "i." Miss Moena did not know much about Moina Michael but Uncle Ben Googled her name and printed her story for Miss Moena. Uncle Ben said every girl and woman should read Moina Michael's story because she was a strong, caring, enduring example of what women can do. Anyhow, Miss Moina Michael was instrumental in beginning the national tradition of selling red poppies on Veterans' Day each year. In World War One, she left her home and job at the State Normal School to go to Washington, DC to help in the war effort. She was too old to go overseas so she remained in Washington where she worked at the National YMCA helping with the war effort. She read the poem "In Flanders Fields" and was so moved by the poem that when the occasion arose she took the opportunity to campaign for the selling of red poppies as a fundraiser for helping disabled war veterans. Today hundreds of millions of dollars have been raised by the Veterans of Foreign Wars to help veterans in need and she is known as the "Poppy Lady." Moina Michael is a Georgian. The State Normal School she left when she went to Washington is today known as the University of Georgia. She came back to UGA to continue to teach. She wrote a poem, "We Shall Keep the Faith," in answer to "In Flanders Fields." She was honored as one of Georgia's most famous women and, a U.S. Postage Stamp was printed in her honor. A bust of Moina Michael is in the rotunda of the Georgia state capitol and a Liberty Ship was named for her after her death in 1944 during World War Two.

Uncle Ben said we probably never would have known about Moina Michael if we had never met Miss Moena.

After we got home Uncle Ben told me I should always listen carefully to older people because they didn't get to be that old by being dumb. He said that although a lot of older people might seem slow to me, they have lived a lot longer and they have a lot more experience in getting through life and almost everything we can learn from them is really valuable. Then he said, "Just look at Aunt Kay. She didn't know that much when I married her but now she's a lot smarter than I am."

The Kensley Report #13 – 2012

The Kensley Report XIII– Today was the laziest day yet. Uncle Ben had a home appraiser come by to appraise the house. The appraiser was out in the wet grass in tennis shoes and when he came in with dirty shoes, Uncle Ben said, "I'll go ahead and hold that clipboard for you while my wife whips you for coming in here with those dirty shoes. She whips me even when she professes to love me so I know she's going to give you a bad beating because she doesn't even know you." The guy looked kind of embarrassed but Uncle Ben told him, "Go ahead and take your shoes off because we have an elderly lady who lives one house over and I don't want her to be scared by that ambulance coming out here to pick you up."

Uncle Ben showed me pictures of a Great Blue Heron, he and the neighbor's son, Andy, captured. The bird had a broken wing caused by an attack from dogs. The four year old girl named Addison who lives one house over said, "What's the bird's name?" Uncle Ben said, "His name is Charley." Addison said, "Charlie is a girl." Uncle Ben said, "Oh." When Uncle Ben is confused or dumbfounded, which is pretty often, he will just say, "Oh." Addison calls him Umple Ben because that's how she learned to say uncle when she was real small. She has a real uncle that she calls uncle but she still calls Uncle Ben, "Umple." Uncle Ben and Andy took Charlie blindfolded in a big box about 70 miles toward Dublin to a woman who rescues animals but Charlie could not be saved because the wing bones are so thin and delicate they often will not mend after being broken.

The air conditioning people came out to service the air conditioning units. When they went up in the attic, Aunt Kay and Uncle Ben told me to get in an area of the house that was not under the section where the a/c guys were in case one of them fell through the ceiling. I thought he was kidding but Uncle Ben says he has a neighbor whose wife went upstairs and stepped in the wrong place and her whole leg came through the ceiling. She was a large woman and when she went to yelling and hollering that she was stuck, her husband and Uncle Ben were outside and they ran in the house in a big panic. They flew upstairs and her husband grabbed her by the arm and went wild trying to yank her loose from the ceiling. Uncle Ben said, "Hold on, don't let her go," and he ran downstairs and got a big pair of vice grip pliers and went down under her and stood on a chair. He said he yelled upstairs, "She's coming out, catch her!" Then he clamped down on her big toe with those vice-grip pliers. Uncle Ben said she snatched her leg out of that hole like a snake had her and her husband broke three of his ribs and her right arm trying to hold her down to keep her from going through the roof. He said they never saw those vice-grip pliers again.

We watched "The Patriot" on TV this afternoon. I told Uncle Ben it makes me nervous when you see those scenes where somebody gets shot or stuck in the throat with a knife and I want to twist my head or jump to one side so they can't get to me. Uncle Ben said he was the same way and when he was a teenager, it got so bad for him that he would start jerking backwards and jumping around in his seat or sliding way down to dodge a bullet, then popping back up to watch the next scene. Sometimes before the movie even got started good the usher would come down the aisle with a flashlight and walk him outside and tell him to go home. He was banned from the Albany Theater until he was 21. He said it was all 3-D to him long before they ever invented 3-D. Uncle Ben has a nice way of making you comfortable with your imaginary fears.

The Kensley Report #14 – 2012

The Kensley Report XIV– I guess if you come to pick me up today this will be my last report to you from Camp Kay. I think Uncle Ben is just getting older. We could not get some of our projects off the ground like we did in past summers and I just heard him tell somebody that he only wears a sock on his right foot because his left foot doesn't like socks. The sock he wears on his right foot is always the same sock and it is a pretty old sock. He said it is a lot older than I am. He also told the guy that he thinks he dislocated his shoulder this afternoon trying to get that old sock off his right foot.

The jewelry marketing scheme fell flat because Uncle Ben says the people at Etsy may be more mentally challenged than he is. Our jewelry pictures look like slides of rabid bacteria fried in bacon fat. He said he's going to fire Etsy because if they propose to have a national or international presence they are absolutely going to have to teach their computers to talk Southern. We couldn't understand their website instructions and he was afraid to call them because he gets tired of talking to people in India who get confused when they answer his call and he yells, "Hey." He always yells, "Hey" when he calls somebody and it really scares and confuses people in India. Anyhow, I am packing up the "jewry" as he calls it to bring home with me.

One of our projects is still pretty much a secret but we will continue to work on it as soon as Uncle Ben can explain it to Paul. Paul knows how to talk to people in India. Paul does not yell, "Hey" when they answer the phone. We were going to make wind chimes from bamboo today but Aunt Kay made Uncle Ben mow the lawn because she got lost in a patch of tall weeds yesterday when we came home from town. She stepped too far out of the car. I never before noticed how short she is.

Uncle Ben did go check some bamboo growing out back but he hurried back in and said we shouldn't go out there because he saw a green mamba crawling in the bamboo. He said they are a highly venomous snake and you can die from the bite. I said, "Green mambas do not live in Southeast Georgia. They live in East Africa." He said, "I just saw one in Southeast Georgia." So I said, "Let's go out there and let me look at him." After we looked around we saw the snake in the bamboo and I said, "Uncle Ben, that is a grass snake and he is harmless. He's probably too scared to bite you and his mouth is so small he can't bite you." Uncle Ben just looked at me and said, "You know Ken Ken, I liked you a lot more before you became both a teen-ager and a Googler." I think Uncle Ben is not only feeling his age, he can't handle the heat anymore. It makes him dizzy.

We watched "Four Weddings" on TV and Uncle Ben loves to comment on the wedding gowns. Yesterday we watched this extremely large girl in a sleeveless wedding gown and Uncle Ben said, "She should not wear a sleeveless gown because her arms look like hams on a #1 Yorkshire sow. They should list her in the National Swine Registry." I said, "Uncle Ben, you are being ugly. She might not be able to control her weight." Uncle Ben said, "You are absolutely right, Ken Ken. Obviously she cannot control her weight. However, a woman with arms that large should fork out another thousand dollars and get some more fabric to cover up all that flesh. She could save a fortune by buying a used parachute for material."

Then I asked Aunt Kay what kind of wedding dress did she have and Aunt Kay showed me their wedding album. My Daddy was the ring bearer and he had curly blonde hair combed over his ears. He was so cute. Uncle Ben and Aunt Kay looked young and pretty. Aunt Kay changed into a dress to travel in and I've got to tell you, it barely covered her bottom. Aunt Kay said girls wore miniskirts and mini dresses in those days and when I exclaimed, "Wow!" Uncle Ben said, "Yes, yes, wasn't it wonderful?"

They told me that they had been married for about five years when, one evening, both families were together enjoying a bird supper, Aunt Kay's mother (Granny) and Uncle Ben's Mother (Mama Ro) discovered, in conversation, that they both descended from Henry Crawford Tucker who was a Colquitt County pioneer and whose claim to fame was he fathered 32 children by three wives. Mama Ro descended from one of Tucker's first children by his first wife and Granny descended from one of his youngest children by his third wife. This means that Aunt Kay and Mama Ro had the same Great, Great Grandfather. Uncle Ben and Aunt Kay were speechless for a while and decided they were about fourth cousins, or so, and that it really didn't matter at this point because they had been married for over five years. But then Paul came along and this meant that Henry Crawford Tucker is Paul's third and also his fourth Great Grandfather. Uncle Ben said they worried for a while when Paul was born and just a baby because it looked like his eyes were sot too close together but after he got a little older, his head got bigger and now his eyes and his head seem to match up okay.

III - DUBIOUS HEALTH TIPS

These health tips come from all over so be sure you do not take them too seriously because who knows if they ever really worked or not. It reminds me of a story I heard about a family that believed watermelon would render rattlesnake bites harmless because one time old Uncle Julius got bitten by a rattlesnake and he had just eaten a slice of watermelon and that old rattlesnake bite never bothered him a bit. They never stopped to consider that the snake can control the amount of poison it injects in you or the snake might have already expended most of its venom on a recent strike. If they really can control the amount of venom they inject when they strike, I'll bet they do that rarely on huge objects, like people. Do not count on eating a slice of watermelon to protect you from a rattlesnake's venom. What worked for old Uncle Julius is not likely to work for you.

I think that most of these tips are truly dubious. Some of them are actually old home remedies that have worked for a number of people over the years but whether or not you would want to try them is totally up to you and if you have a doctor or a physician's assistant you normally see, you might want to run anything out of the ordinary by them before you try something that we have dubbed dubious. That adjective should make you suspicious right from the start.

Dubious Health Tips #1 – Fighting Back! Fighting Arthritis!

I think Katie Mae and I beat the allergies that attacked when we moved north of the gnat line to Athens, Georgia. We whipped the allergies but, the doldrums struck us and we became totally listless. We slowly came out of listlessness and improved to the stage of worthlessness. Then there came a near-complete recovery to the point of, "not-worth-killing." I told my old friend C.Tross that the "not-worth-killing" level makes me feel young again. I can remember when we were teenagers, Chan Chandler's Dad and my Dad joined voices in a chorus of critical comments (about the status of Chan and me and our unmitigated laziness) culminating in their declaration that a drop of sweat from either of us, mixed in a number-three washtub full of creek water, would kill every mosquito in Dougherty County. That was our "not-worth-killing" period.

Now I am old and back to the not-worth-killing stage. I can't include Katie Mae because she still goes like a buzz-saw every day. I keep checking her meds to see if she is hiding the good stuff from me but I guess it's all a natural high with her. None of my prescriptions are capable of propelling me into that jet stream she lives in.

Dubious Health Tip #1 – Fighting Back

That big joint where the thumb bone is connected to the hand bone draws me closer to the Lord every morning when

I have to drag my hands out of bed. I never heard Ezekiel mention that bone when singing "Dry Bones" and I think it was because, like me, Ezekiel never worked in the fields. He missed the most important bone in the body. That thumb is about the only thing that distinguishes man from all the monkeys and most species of skunk.

I understand the big joint in your thumb is one of several carpometacarpal (CMC) joints that you have in your hand. This joint is said to be biaxial which is an obscure Latin term for having someone hack each of your thumbs two times with an ax. My hands feel like somebody beat me on the back of them with the bottom of a golf shoe but I couldn't possibly have carpal tunnel syndrome because the only repetitive thing I have done consistently over the years is twist the tops off beer bottles and peanut butter jars.

Recently, when the pain reached near-unbearable, I dug through a drawer of old outdated salves and elixirs and came up with a tube of capsaicin. Capsaicin, for those of you who don't know, is made from an extract of hot chili peppers. Some brands may be a synthetic reproduction of the extract but you get my drift. This stuff will burn the cheeks right off your fanny! Be sure you do not use it on your fanny.

I gingerly rubbed this super simmering salve on the backs of my tormented thumbs with great caution in an attempt to keep it off my fingers and palms. Then I washed just the insides of my hands, palms and fingers and carefully dried them.

This was great! It worked! It worked! It worked for all of ten seconds!

In no time I had a generous smear of the blistering fires from hell across my upper lip, my right cheek and my left eyelid. All were still burning several hours later. That night, when I took a shower, my hands lit up like a couple of those old fashioned railroad lanterns.

When I looked for some sympathy from Kay she said, "Why did you put it on your lips? I didn't realize you had arthritis in your lips. Doesn't arthritis usually affect bones and joints? Surely you don't have any bones or joints in your lips, do you? I don't remember anything about the lip bone being connected to the head bone!"

After listening to all that, I was really burned up! I thought seriously about manually defending myself from such demeaning statements. I quickly reconsidered when I thought bigger lips would mean bigger pain for me. If she gave me a little love tap on my mouth my lips could be a lot fatter. More fat could mean more pain. I remained silent.

Apparently she has forgotten the once irresistible attraction of my lips and their handsomely sculptured, undeniably kissable appeal.

I have a suggestion to anyone who chooses to use capsaicin. Enlist the aid of friends. Have them dress in nuclear, biological, chemical cleanup suits. When they have finished slathering you in capsaicin, they can swath you in layers of bindings that will leave you looking like an Egyptian mummy. Be prepared to relive scenes from Dante's Inferno. If you survive we want to hear of your experiences while you were aflame and blazing in the mummy suit. Some of us might want to reevaluate our religious views.

Be careful with capsaicin. I think its original use was for treatment of arthritic crocodiles and cracked toe nails on elephants.

I once read that a cardiologist looking for a good diet for his heart patients came up with something that also aided in decreasing the pain of arthritis. He said it would benefit us greatly if we would consume more chlorophyll. He suggested a glass of frozen wheat grass or green barley each day. Well, this may work fine for you but I keep thinking all that grass consumption will keep me closely and constantly anchored to the bathroom and every time I pass that bathroom mirror, I'm going to be taking a peek to see if I have grown horns or if I am beginning to resemble one of those cows on the Chick-Fil-A commercials.

And let me tell you something else about getting old. The torment of getting old ain't always about the pain of arthritis. If your sweet darling is not sympathetic with the pain you endure from arthritis, your feelings can be terribly hurt. Hurt or crushed feelings can also leave you with terminal drag-ass. I had to add that because Katie Mae hurt my feelings by making fun of my scorched lip problem.

Dubious Health Tips #2 – Your Ear Is Not A Candle Holder!

If you are as far from reality as I sometimes get, I'll bet you had no idea that some people are actually going to spas or ear-candling parlors to have the wax removed from their ears by other people who, like them, are also lacking in good sense. This procedure is supposed to draw wax out of your ears and involves the placing of a cone-shaped device in your ear canal. The device is activated by a burning wick or smoke which will drain wax and other impurities from inside your ear.

You can get colored candles, scented candles and for the purists you can get candles made of pure beeswax rather than the more common paraffin candles. Some of this is undoubtedly for people with discriminating ears. I'm sure my ears would be offended if I did not use pure beeswax in a bright color with a pleasing periwinkle scent. My ears can tell the difference. I often use them for smelling when my nose gets bent out of shape.

These people will tell you this coning practice began in ancient times in China, Tibet and India. You should remember the life expectancy in those countries back then was about thirty years and if you go around doing stupid things to your body like burning candles in your ear, you can expect to add about one more week, beginning today, to the length of your life.

Some of them actually think the ear canal is connected to your sinuses, your lymph glands and even your brain. I know for a fact that if you are burning candles in your ears, you do not have a brain so you can forget about cleansing something you do not have. The truth is the fire and smoke does not create a vacuum in your ear canal strong enough to extract earwax. Earwax is thick and viscous. If you created a vacuum in your ear strong enough to suck the wax out, your eardrum would be snatched right out stuck to a hunk of earwax.

You never know where your own personal danger may be lurking. Remember if you are trying this, we have established you have no brain. If you have no brain, there is already a vacuum in your head. Creating an opposing vacuum with an ear candle, will result in an implosion that will make your nose swell up to the size of a grapefruit. This happens just before your head caves in.

Do not put a cone in your ear and light it! It is extremely dangerous. There are cases of people having to make emergency room trips to get treatment for their burnt ears. The ear canals on some of these idiots have been horribly burned. Some people had wax stuck to their eardrums. Doctors had to scrape the wax from their eardrums. The eardrum can be perforated and render you permanently deaf. The wax produced by these fakers at the end of such a session did not come out of someone's ear. The residue you might be shown as proof of the cleaning effect of the candle is wax and ashes from the candle and wick. It is candle wax, you dummy, not earwax.

As you probably know, your ears get larger as you age and they may not be as attractive as you once thought but generally they look pretty good tacked to your head right where the Lord chose to stick them. Be sure you hang on to your ears. Do not let an ear-candler transform your ears into charcoal briquettes.

Nothing is mentioned by the ear-candlers that auricular candling or coning, as they call it, has a horrific downside. They really shouldn't have to point it out. We are old and supposedly wise. One of the very first things we ever learned was, "Fire is hot. It will burn the hell out of you!" If you burned yourself in a thoughtless moment as a child, your Momma or Daddy would often add to the blaze by putting some more fire of a different kind in the seat of your britches!

So you are supposed to know from the earliest moments you began walking that fire is extremely dangerous.

I know you won't believe this but several people who have tried ear-candling are no longer with us. That's right. They burned their own fannies up, ears and all. They started out with a serious ear-cleaning mission on their feeble minds but the results were just the same as though they were only three years old and had foolishly played with matches. A woman in Alaska set her bed on fire and then the whole room went up in flames. They got her out, and to the hospital but she later succumbed to an asthma attack.

My own Aunt Dash tried candling recently and the end result was the near devastation of her living room. Her son Orville had put the cone in her ear and lit it but he didn't have her head tilted at the right angle. The candle was too close to her face and a wisp of hair touched the flame. Fortunately they saw it burning in time to brush it away and it fell from her head without burning her. Unfortunately the cat, Topography, was underfoot and the wisp of burning hair landed on Topography's head. He went into a frenzy and was running in circles. His flaming head set the carpet and drapes on fire. They got him out the back door and threw him in an open well.

Aunt Dash had to renovate and refurbish her entire living room. Orville fished Topography out of the well but the cat may never grow back all that hair he lost off his big head. He is one embarrassed bald-headed cat nowadays. He won't even come out from under the bed in the back bedroom to eat. Aunt Dash has to slide his food under the bed. The cat was named Lucky. Since he caught fire and lost the hair on his head, Orville has renamed him Topography. He has a birthmark on top of his head that looks like an outline of Australia. I'm not sure about the mark. It could be a big blister.

I hope this helped you. Just remember, ear wax is natural. It usually dissipates naturally. You do not have to dig with a pickax and shovel in your ear to dislodge it. If you think you have a problem see a doctor. Remember what old Doctor

Rhine used to tell us. "Never put anything smaller than your elbow in your ear."

I'll bet at this point you are standing in front of a mirror. You're standing there looking at your elbow and your ear!

Dubious Health Tips #3 – Things You Probably Shouldn't Do!

I am frantically searching for things that will make old people feel better inside their own skins and that should pretty much cover your whole body. There are remedies out there but when I mention one here, I want you to rest assured that I have no earthly idea if the remedy will kill you or cure you. I entertain strange health tips and ideas because I often hurt like hell. I am certainly not above dreaming myself back to feeling good....if dreaming will work......who knows? Try these at your own risk. I will do my best to forewarn you if I think the remedy is whacko crazy or makes sense to me.

When I say "Makes Sense to me," I want you to realize that I do not have a lot of sense. I think the first time I took an IQ test in high school my score was the same number of inches as Katie Mae is tall. She is sixty one and one-half inches tall. The teacher did not give me the half-inch on my score so I came out with a 61 which is about twenty points below moronic.

The last time I took an IQ test I upped the ante a little because during that six year span, I had read a book. My score was the same number as the room temperature. It was a pretty chilly day and we had no heat in the classroom. My score was 65. You can see from those scores that you are dealing with a poor soul who has not been blessed with a full deck of cards. Be aware that I write about this stuff because I may think it is fantastic or I may think it is bizarre. Usually I don't believe any of it will keep us free of pain much longer than a nano second.

Onion – You can cut up an onion into chunks and place them in strategic places around the house. Don't ask me where a strategic place is. If Katie Mae catches me wasting onions and if the smell lingers more than an hour or if she catches me stashing onions around her house (you notice I said, "Her house") there will be no strategic places for me to hide. They say the onion chunks will absorb bugs like flu bugs and other clandestine bacteria lurking in odd corners. They also say the smell will clear up a stuffy nose. I might add, the smell can also ward off unwelcome visits from friends and relatives thereby keeping your home free of obnoxious house guests.

Potato and Fevers – Slice a potato and soak the slices in vinegar. Place the slices on your forehead. Be sure you are lying down. It's hard to keep the potato slices on your forehead if you are standing unless you can bear the pain of using thumb tacks. You can stand if you have that high forehead so many of my old friends have attained. If your better half is thrifty like Katie Mae, wasting potatoes can shorten your life span. Your head will be broken before your fever breaks. Getting your head broken is the penalty for wasting potatoes in my house. Potatoes ain't cheap anymore. If you find this cure has worked for you, be sure you wash the vinegar from your forehead afterward. You can wind up with the same desirable or not-so-desirable results that you got from using the onions. The smell of vinegary potatoes wafting through the house will leave you all alone, whether you want to be or not.

Tennis Balls and Sore Feet – This one is really crazy. Put the tennis balls on the floor and roll your tired, sore feet over the balls. Take your shoes off first. They also say that a frozen bottle of water works well if your feet are hot and tired. I say this is all wrong. You know how we love to nap! You could fall into a deep sleep with your feet resting on tennis balls. When the phone rings or she calls you to supper you will leap up! You will be trying to walk on tennis balls! The injuries resulting from the nasty spill you take will spin you into about a three to four month recovery period. Getting all those unnatural curves and kinks out of your spine takes time!

They also don't bother to mention that the ice in the bottle will melt and leave condensation all over the floor. This is another excellent way to toss your body (wretched back included) against the far wall. If you foolishly decide to try using tennis balls and frozen bottles of water, remember to remain seated. Do not stand. If you use the frozen bottle method, go ahead and get the mop out. You don't think anybody is going to clean up your big sloppy mess, do you?

Body Brushes – Brush the dead skin that clogs your pores with a body brush before you bathe. Brushing toward your heart will improve your circulation. This also helps you save money because you can use less deodorant by doing a prebath brush down. This is nuts! I use a wash cloth which is all you need to remove dead cells and skin as you bathe.

Using a body brush on your dry hide is going to leave it red and raw all over. Brushing around your heart creates a monster nipple. Your left nipple will be raw, angry and infuriated with you. You'll be stuck in a closet for a week reading bad novels because you cannot put clothes on the monster nipple until it heals. That part about using less deodorant is simply a repeat of the other advice and you will be right back to chasing off your friends and loved ones because you smell like a goat.

Try what you like! I personally think these suggestions were written by a misanthrope, a person who dislikes other people. It's obvious that most of what's written here will run off friends, relatives, and neighbors. Try these suggestions and you'll be lucky if you can get your dog to stay home.

Dubious Health Tips #4 – Arthritis – Something that Might Really Work!

I'm back on the pain of my life. It's the Thumbo pain and like Dumbo's ears, it is a pain that is so big it has my body and my soul in its torturous grip. This is the same pain in the thumb bones I desperately tried to squelch by using capsaicin. Capsaicin is a salve containing hot chili pepper extract that burned parts of me unmercifully. Read all about it in Health Tips #1.

Health Tips #1 was written to be humorous (I think) but this new (#4) health tip is actually serious. It might even work for some folks. I'm convinced it would work for me if I would stick to the program at least two or three times a week. Unfortunately, it involves a ritual and I hate rituals. Free spirits like us should not be bound by rituals.

This one health tip that might actually work for some people is partly an old folk remedy. It's Castor Oil. I know it's weird but I believe it would work if I would do this at least three times a week. My problem is I am lazy and the lazy is stronger than the thumb pain. My unorthodox strategy is to rub the Castor Oil into the backs of my thumbs until most of the oily part has worked its way into the skin. That is as far as the old folk remedy goes.

Then I put on rubber gloves that you use for cleaning. This is not part of the old folk remedy. I've got some gloves called home helpers. I also use some from Mr. Clean called

"Loving Hands." They are yellow and have the long cuffs. This is important (long cuffs) because you want to be sure the oil on your hands stays inside the gloves. You will live longer this way. If your little woman is a neat freak your hands will never get better. When you leave a lot of oil smudges around the house she'll rap your aching knuckles with an old broom stick. She'll hit you so hard you'll think you're back in Miss Henderson's third grade classroom.

This is the third step I take. I have a pair of (get this) mittens that are made just like a heating pad. You plug in one wire but you have a mitten for each hand. You can keep warming one hand while you work the remote control with the other. The yellow gloves keep the oil off everything. You can't imagine how wonderful your hands will feel with those heated mittens on them. I use the lowest temperature setting and the great thing about this method is you can turn off the heated mittens, slip your gloved hands out and go to the bathroom or wherever you like and then return to the healing warmth of the mittens. You can use your fingers once you slip off the mittens and the Castor Oil will stay inside the gloves and not on your poor wife's favorite furniture.

The mittens are manufactured by Jilbere de Paris and something makes me think they are for girls and women but I don't care. They make me one happy boy. When I have those warm gloves on I feel like I can survive a few more days without that constant infernal pain clawing at my hands.

I also have a Jilbere de Paris paraffin heater. I put Castor Oil in the wax. Is seems to work for me. The paraffin heater does not have a thermostat. It has only the on/off switch and the wax can get too hot so you have to use care to avoid blistering your fingers with melted wax. You don't want to lose your favorite digits. The wax is pretty expensive and you're supposed to discard the wax once you have tortured your hands with it.

Gloves are also available that have no fingers for use by arthritis sufferers. They are supposed to be energizing and therapeutic support gloves but I don't think they work for me. I have a pair of them and when you put this kind of glove on it leaves your fingers naked. I was born with shy fingers. If I have to go see who rang the doorbell, I'm in trouble with my half-naked fingers. I notice immediately that the visitor's eyes go directly to my hands with the fingerless gloves. My super embarrassed fingers turn a bright red. I just can't wear something that indecent!

They say magnets stop pain. I am going to begin studying magnets and their effects on the pain we get from arthritis. Geezer Grit will report our findings in a future blog. I know a number of people who have used magnets and they swear they work but I am a bit skeptical. You can carry anything too far and simply overdo it.

My friend Bubba Jack Johnson's mother lived alone. She had gone all-out and become a magnet fanatic. She used the magnetic cure for everything that ailed her. She had a magnetic bed and magnetic pillow covers. She bought a case of different sized magnetic bandages that she used every time she got a little twinge in a joint.

The last straw occurred when Bubba Jack, after not hearing from his Mama for two days, went to her house and found her stuck to the refrigerator.

After he managed to pry her off the fridge with a crow bar, he threw all her magnets away.

Dubious Health Tips #5 – Aloe Infused Socks

You totally missed the International Day of Older Persons. It occurred on the first of October. There was a huge hoopla and ballyhoo! Missed it, didn't you? You're getting older and you miss a lot these days. I wouldn't worry too much if I were you. It was sponsored by the United Nations and since most of their programs cost Americans billions of dollars and produce nothing but trouble for us and the rest of the world, it's good we didn't worry with it. I lied about the hoopla and ballyhoo. I heard nothing about it either. That's typical for a UN undertaking.

But I do think there is something you are really missing. You should pay more attention to the things going on around you that might be helpful and healthy for you.

If you are like most geezers and geezerettes, you are spending way too much time waiting in line at your pharmacy for prescriptions that might work or might not work. You're not sure which ones are working either, are you? Use that waiting time to check out the aisles in the pharmacy. You will be astonished to see all the wonderful new products the stores are stocking just to keep you in sparkling good health.

Dubious Health Tips #5 - Today I saw a rack full of aloe-infused multicolored socks. I'm not sure what aloe-infused socks will do for you but, admittedly, the possibilities are never ending. To tell the truth, they did not look like socks. They were not shaped like feet. I first thought they were some kind of interchangeable bra cups for an elderly woman who was extremely thin and who had once breast fed over twenty some-odd children. If they really were socks they looked like they were made for a very tiny person with no ankles.

They were a horrible day-glow orange color with raggedy yellow polka-dots. The little tag on the socks said they were made in France. My bet was they were made in China and foisted off on the French who will go for just about anything that looks fashionably appalling. The proof is right there in those ugly socks that France owes China a lot of money. I sure hope we don't owe China that much money!

The real question is, "What do you do with aloe infused socks?" If you have some exotic foot problem you might decide to wear them to bed and while you're sleeping you could lose one of the socks. Are you in trouble? You bet, if the socks are slick and you have a hardwood floor. When the alarm clock begins that early morning auricular madness, you will jump out of bed in a flash. The sock that is still on your foot hits the floor; your foot slides from under you and you go into a tailspin like a duck landing on an icy pond. You do a double back flip and crash on that hardwood floor. When you regain consciousness you will find a giant goose egg on that slick, bald head of yours. Your back and butt will be jacked into several opposing ninety degree angles. The resulting scream from your tortured lips will prove to your disbelieving bride that you actually do have a falsetto voice as good as Frankie Valli's.

On the other hand (or foot) if one sock comes off and the other one stays put the aloe on the remaining sock will have softened your foot to the consistency of jello. When you step out of bed you won't be able to feel the softened foot touch the floor. Your torso, including all attachments, will continue moving forward into a disastrous topple which will flip you over and throw you into a tailspin like a duck landing on an icy pond (you know the rest of that sad story, so just use your imagination).

The very least that could happen to you is not good either. If you get out of bed and the aloe anointed sock has only slightly softened your foot, it will take two hours of walking in a circle before feeling returns and you can walk in a straight line. This feeling returns right after you had to pee down your leg because you couldn't walk straight to the bathroom. Since you peed down the numb leg you didn't know you were urinating. Don't worry, the supreme ruler of your home will soon be in to check on you and she will discover a big wet spot on the floor. Next will come the humiliation you'll suffer by catching hell for being so shiftless and lazy. You sorry rascal! You peed on the floor instead of walking ten feet to the bathroom.

Let all of this be a warning to you about trying something as dumb as aloe-infused socks. If by now, after you have been so earnestly and truthfully warned, you are still convinced you need aloe-infused socks just send me an e-mail. I bought ten pairs of the damned things. You can have mine.....Cheap!!

Dubious Health Tips #6 – How are you handling Old?

How are you handling Old? Old tends to beat you up and it always wins in the end but I keep looking for ways to fight back. I'm never sure if I win a battle so I keep comparing myself with other old geezers who are still able to shuffle around. I think I am in better shape than a lot of them. Sometimes I find that I am muttering under my breath about what age some guy might be. He may look old but then I realize that I am much older than him. I also realize how hard it is to mutter under your breath when you're always short on air. When you run out of breath, you tend to fall down and that's embarrassing and painful. Don't mutter under your breath.

I have a myriad of health problems but I have been blessed by the Angel of Moderation. She has always been with me. There's no proof like living proof and, despite all odds, I'm still alive. The Angel of Moderation seems to temper the pain (most of the time) from arthritis, prostate problems, asthma, peripheral neuropathy, scoliosis, degenerative vertebrae, being half blind, managing juke joints in my misspent youth and so many other disorders that listing them all would bore you to your last teardrop and you probably have more afflictions than I do.

In time I have tried a number of weird remedies for my ailments and subsequent pain, none of which have seemed to work but I would like to share one with you. Later you can curse me for telling you this if you try it and it doesn't work.

If it works, you can say a pain-whupping prayer for me. And please say a prayer for my Angel who has to listen to me curse when the pain wins. She is the same Angel that usually allows me to suffer in moderation rather than total misery.

Dubious Health Tips #6 - Dancing Your Way Back

I just read you can dance your way to better health. This is just true for one person in Georgia. That person is Jerry Hobbs. I often refer to Hobbs as Lester Lightfoot (just to myself). Jerry/Lester got in shape recently; first, by losing over a hundred pounds riding a three wheeled bicycle around St. Simons Island, Georgia and the adjoining islands (just to the islands that have bridges to the mainland – the bicycle does not work well in the surf). I think Jerry has been cycling for about 300 miles a day and then, by evening light, he Shags his ass off (literally) with old women all over the Golden Isles of Georgia. Lester was a world class dancer in his youth back in Albany, Georgia where we all grew to what we mistakenly thought was adulthood. Remember now, Lester is still a world class dancer and, more importantly, you are not.

The article also mentioned dancing can protect you against dementia, diabetes and high blood pressure. First of all, let's talk dementia. If you have dementia you should not be out there dancing. You'll forget what dance you're doing and you will try to change gears at high speed. You'll throw that super expensive hip replacement joint right through a wall. Nobody will be safe. And another thing; some of those old Shag dancers are mean. If dementia strikes you in mid-Shag-step and you forget where you are, you'll be abandoned in the middle of the dance floor. You see, they have dementia too. The police will have to figure out who you are and where you live.

You can also forget about dancing to help control your diabetes. I know how you love to dance and drink beer and eat glazed donuts at the same time. I've seen you do it! Snarfing down donuts and drinking cold beer while dancing does not help a diabetic condition. You will get big blisters on those ugly feet of yours and they will not heal. And as far as helping your blood pressure, forget about that too. Dancing with old people does not lower your blood pressure. Old people are extremely cranky and they bitch and moan a lot, especially when they're dancing. They are just pretending to have fun. They can't remember what fun was all about. Their bodies will be in great pain. They will blame you for all that pain and after they are through chewing you out for making them hurt so much, your blood pressure will skyrocket. Don't do it!

Do not try this. Do not think dancing is going to be your great salvation. Dancing has only been good for Lester Lightfoot and he was an excellent dancer when he was a child, besides, all the old widows and single women at St. Simons Island are in love with, "Lester Lightfoot, the Skillful Shag Dancing Senior." They give him foot rubs and full body massages every day. I believe all that sweet attention is going to give an incredible boost to his chances of living to be over one hundred. His example is not a good one for you to follow. You'll never make it by trying the Lester Lightfoot method!

Once again, do not try dancing to make you healthier. You will wind up with cartilage scattered all over the dance floor and enough loose ligament and tendons to make custom shoelaces for Shaquille O'Neal's basketball shoes.

Don't risk the pain! Stay safe! Sit on the sidelines, drink your cold beer, eat your glazed donuts and die happily in your sleep.

Dubious Health Tips #7 – Self Preservation – Practice Lyming

If you are trying to hang on to whatever it is you have left (body or soul), you have got to stay alert. Watch what's happening around you. You young boomers can use me as a gauge. If you see me slowing down and taking more naps, then you should follow suit. As long as I make that daily wakeup call and I manage to stand up fairly straight, you have a good example to follow. Laugh as much and as loud and as long as you can! If I fall over dead, do not continue to use me as a gauge. At that point I will have set a bad example for you. Watch what's going on around you. Some of this weird stuff can be good for you.

Watching and reading is how I learned about lyming. Lyming is the fine old Caribbean art of doing absolutely nothing. I feel very strongly that we old timers should begin to practice lyming immediately but most of us already know how to lyme. Make this a daily practice with no serious interruptions except for tragedies in your immediate vicinity, like a loved one falling down the stairs or a car running over you.

The secret is to Lyme artistically and creatively. Position your body on a couch or bed so your folks will know you are creatively lyming. If you don't do this correctly they might think you are shuffling off the old mortal coil. They will try to give you a quick and double dose of defibrillation to revive you. This could come to you as a bit of a shock and it could have the opposite effect by turning out your lights.

I believe I was born to Lyme. I remember ordering hammocks made in Mexico years before Uncle Skip gave me a Pawley's Island, multi-person hammock. My Mexican, one man, hammock I complemented with a colorful steel rod topped with a whirling circular holder just the right size for a beer can. You stabbed the rod in the ground. You needed the holder on the side of the hammock where you kept your beer gripping hand.

I could spend hours in that hammock with the only downside being I had to occasionally get up to retrieve another cold beer from the cooler and put it in the beer holder. This was years before my prostate took over my bladder functions and a long time before I began to have conversations with my prostate gland. I could go make water when I wanted to.

Back then they claimed alcohol killed brain cells so I had to watch the amount I consumed. I knew brain cells in my head were a rarity and I couldn't afford to kill many. I calculated the ratio to be one twelve ounce beer per sacrificial brain cell. By my calculation I could cerebrally afford to drink two six packs before napping. It got really tricky after eight or ten beers trying to gracefully slip from the hammock without spinning myself into a cocoon. This was extremely dangerous because once entrapped in something resembling a butterfly's first home, Katie Mae would leave me there for several days.

Now I'm an old hand at Lyming. I don't use hammocks anymore. I can Lyme anywhere I happen to be standing. I'm Lyming right now. All I have to do to stop Lyming and return to what I was doing is wipe the drool off this keyboard. Give it a shot. It can't hurt you unless, of course, you are supposed to be doing yard work or the dishes.

Don't Be Such a Wuss! Get the Flu Shot!

I used to manage truck lines. It was unbelievable the number of big old tough truck drivers who would go to mumbling and moaning about having to take a shot to prevent the flu and, sure enough, most of them would not get the shot. They would swear that every time they had the shot, they would get sick with a bad cold or even the flu. I'm sure some folks have a bad reaction to flu shots but most of these guys were indulging in girly man needle fright. After all, the flu shot is an "inactivated" vaccine. That means the vaccine is "dead" folks! Dead vaccines do not hurt you, unless of course you have already convinced yourself that it's going to kill you. Then it will probably kill you!

Now the reason I brought all this up is we now have a flu shot that's much stronger than the one they give younger folks. I did not know this and I'm thinking you might not know it either. There is a shot for people 65 or older. It's called the Fluzone High-Dose Seasonal Influenza Vaccine and you old timer cowboy truck drivers can rest easy now in the sure knowledge that this shot will kick your ass. You won't have to make up wussy stories about flu shots making you sick anymore. The Fluzone High-Dose vaccine contains four times the amount of antigen that is in regular flu shots. It is supposed to give you stronger immune responses and old geezers and geezerettes like us need that extra immunity. The shot, as I said, really knocked me on my fanny so I went to bed earlier than usual. I was positive that I had pneumonia and all three of the influenzas the shot was designed to prevent. I got up the next morning feeling great. This flu shot was tough on me but only for one evening.

If the needle scares you, don't watch. I know some of these nurses who give you the shot are impatient and they're ready for five o'clock. As soon as they leave work they go down to Bill's Bawdy Billiards and toss back a few beers while they play darts. That's how they practice giving flu shots. Years ago I was one of the original needle-cowards but if I can handle this shot the rest of you can too. Did I mention this shot will kick your ass? It kicked mine but the next morning, I was as good as I am ever going to get.

Beware the "SOBIN!"

The third tip I picked up a couple of days ago is one that you might use to preserve your bank account, sanity, and peace of mind; not necessarily in that order.

Be aware, especially during the Thanksgiving and Christmas season, of scammers and other unscrupulous people who are out there just lurking in the shadows ready to jump out and take advantage of us (the aged). Scientists have just discovered that the reason we are so easy to scam as we get older is a physical change in our brain that makes us less discerning and less suspicious of people who are lying to us.

A part of your brain called the "Insular Cortex" grows cold, so to speak, and it does not flare up in recognition of certain signals that, at one time, would warn us when a dishonest bum was telling us a lie.

Watch out for them. Protect yourself when you are dealing with someone you don't know well. You you might try using a mantra to make you more alert. A mantra is a sound, syllable or group of words capable of creating a spiritual transformation in you when you use it appropriately. I say my mantras silently to myself. I use an off-prescription method in some of my mantras. When I am dealing with someone I suspect of wrongdoing, I use the mantra, "WOUTSOBIN." It is pronounced "WHAT SOBIN." I say it silently over and over to myself. It means "Watch OUT, SOB Is Near!!!"

You might not know what a mantra is but I'll bet you know what an SOB is!

Take care of yourself.

Dubious Health Tips #8 - Scent Therapy, One Way to Take It Off!

There is a weigh out there for you to lose weight without spending an arm and a leg but it might benefit some of you really big'uns to go ahead and sacrifice a couple of limbs for the sake of saving the rest of your body. I just read a helpful little tip about distracting yourself if hunger throws you into a full-blown spin-out. Do something that gets your undivided attention for a few minutes until your craving passes. I decided to fling myself head first into the nearest wall as a perfect distraction and it seemed to be working until I passed out. I got off the floor a few minutes ago. My head is hurting like hell and I am twice as hungry because of all that physical stuff like indiscriminate body flinging.

I decided that distracting and flinging is not for me. I think about food longingly and lovingly and my devotion to food and its life-sustaining properties is constant. Insulin tells your body when to eat. My insulin is a real chatterbox and I have begun to wonder if they can't put a stint in my fat fanny somewhere so I can tap into my endless insulin supply. Plenty of diabetics have to give themselves insulin shots every day and I just happen to have gallons of it on hand. I'll bet there is a lucrative market for insulin out there. If it is so easy to tap into the source, why can't we push a little insulin straight to the buyers and bypass those greedy pharmaceutical companies, at least until it becomes illegal. By then we should all be pretty well set, financially, and we won't have to worry too much about an abundance of the stuff. We'll keep selling it on the sly.

Anyhow, that's a thought for a future entrepreneurial venture but for now we've got to reduce the lard that so famously girdles our bountiful bodies.

There is a doctor named William Hirsch who is the neurological director of the Smell and Taste Treatment and Research Foundation in Chicago. I assume all this is still true. It has been a few years since I read this article about him and his research.

Dr Hirsch says that if you lose your sense of smell you are very likely to gain too much weight. He also says if overweight people can sniff the aroma of food, they will lose weight. He studied over 3,000 fat people (my words for fat people) who were each given an inhaler that smelled like peppermint, banana, or apple. They had to sniff the inhaler whenever they felt hungry. This research was done over a six month period and though some folks would sniff it as few as 20 times a day, there were a number of these hogs who were hitting the old inhaler 300 times daily. Overall they lost an average of 30 pounds each.

I think nobody knows my strange body like I do. The serious food cravings I have, every waking moment, brings to my mind some serious questions about the scent therapy. One of their theories is, "Sniffing food somehow tricks the brain into thinking that the body is actually consuming food." My brain has been weak since birth and it has become more feeble recently with encroaching age but my weak and feeble brain has never, never, never been tricked into thinking I was actually eating something when I was not stuffing food into my mouth.

Another theory is, "Inhaling a pleasant food aroma helps eliminate the subtle anxiety that often causes people to overeat." I don't know who came up with that phrase "subtle anxiety," but I can tell you there is nothing "subtle" about my, quest-for-food anxiety. I become grizzly bear ravenous and you best not step between me and the chow when the food scent hits my nostrils. Sometimes a gluttonous anxiety hits me and I get physically ill if I can't dive headlong into the grits. Most of the time I eat like a pig because I am a pig and scent has little to do with it.

Doctor Hirsch and his group are well intended and I don't doubt that scent therapy can help people, I just don't happen to be one of those people.

A couple of suggestions his research provided that might aid you in controlling your diet was to sniff and inhale your food deeply before you begin to eat and to chew your food thoroughly. They say the more thoroughly you chew your food, the more scent is liberated. They also advised if you can get away with it at the table, that you try blowing bubbles into your food. This way you can maximize the mixing of the food molecules with air molecules.

I don't know about you and your dining partners, but if I start sniffing my food like an old hound dog at Katie Mae's table, I'm going to have to learn how to eat.... with no teeth... after she takes most of them out with one punch. By the same token, if I spit on Katie Mae or her clean table while blowing bubbles into my food, I will have been slapped.... under the table.... where I can eat the rest of my meal on the floor..... with no teeth.

I'm curious about this scent therapy. I might try it, only when I'm far away from home. I suspect some of the folks in the study went into a food frenzy mode and chewed up the inhalers or swallowed them whole. The study doesn't mention this. Another thing, Doctor Hirsch and his research group must have done this famous study in Chicago. We are in the deep, deep South and I can tell you if you start walking around sniffing on a little inhaler 300 times a day, the narc squad is going to bring a big dog around so he can stick his nose up your fanny to check you out. You are definitely going to look suspicious. Don't do this down South!

Dubious Dietary Deliverance

It's wonderful in America how each new day produces something generated by brilliant minds that will change our way of life and by, "our way of life," you know I'm talking about food.

If you still have a couple of spare tires around what used to be your waist and you seriously need some willpower help in cutting back your calorie consumption, then you have just hit your special day of Dietary Deliverance.

The same guy who invented the Segway has a new group of think-tankers who recently announced the invention of a personal stomach pump. It's called the AspireAssist and it will suck partially digested food right out of your stomach. Famished body parts, other than your stomach, may be begging for a straight-line fat injection but that is not the way the AspireAssist works. You can now have the amazing ability to practically think yourself thin while, at the same time, robbing those starving extremities of 30% of the life producing sustenance you just consumed.

You heard it right! You can retrieve 30% of the food you just ate by pumping it back out. After you pump the food out you've got to shoot some water back in there so everything still lingering in your round-house remains loosey goosey. This seems unbelievable and there are considerations to be considered before you spring for the pump.

Consider this: You have to get a surgically implanted port so you can hook up the pump. That's how they get the cast-away chow out of your stomach. They call it a Skin-Port but I'll bet you it is not made from skin. You will have a plastic tube sticking out of your belly button. That might be a problem for anybody who is in their mid-seventies. By now you may be an old bag with a lot of little bags attached to your aging torso. Another parasitic bag at this point would be a less than attractive option for you.

Consider this: The present downside of the gadget is it can't break up large foods. Foods that clog the system include chips, cauliflower, pretzels, broccoli, and Chinese food. I think if you can't eat Chinese Food you might as well swear off eating any food at all and what about fat Chinese people? What are they going to do? Why can't they have a pump?

Consider this: The inventor Dean Kamen is the same guy who invented the Segway. He probably made a big chunk of change when Segway, Inc. was sold to a wealthy British entrepreneur. The Brit had owned the company only a few months when he drove his personal Segway over a cliff and into a river. He did not make it out alive. That could be an ominous omen.

Consider this: Dean Kamen's father was an illustrator for Mad Magazine, Weird Science and EC Comics. You've just got to believe that the sense of humor in the Kamen household was extremely offbeat, peculiar and bizarre. If you don't think Dean Kamen is weird, Google his name and read about the house he lives in. I like it. I think it's great but it is also thoroughly and utterly strange.

To give Mr. Kamen some credit for his ingenuity I think we ought to mention advantages of his odd invention. The future will see this as an acceptable feeding tool and millions of on-the-go people are going to want one. Think of the time you will save when you rush through a train station or airport and you don't have time for a sit down meal. You go to a vending machine and drop in two or three dollars and a small tube of food will pop out. As soon as you get to your traveling seat, you unbutton the tiny flap on your special order shirt, uncover your Skin Port and you zap a meal right directly into your stomach. The purchased food tube is totally compatible with the Skin Port and is made with its own pump. You pump your MRE* right straight into your stomach and then discard the food tube/pump. You won't get peanuts on the plane but peanut butter and jelly in a tube should be an easy fix.

Millions upon millions of dollars will be saved by people who no longer need extensive dental work because of wear and tear on their teeth. Esophageal reflux and the purple pill will be a thing of the past and bad breath may be blown away. The benefits are far too many to mention here but I'm sure you are already thinking of how easy it will be to prepare meals and to take 30% of what you have already eaten right off the top.

Consider this: I feel pretty sure that Mr. Kamen is moving too fast for our generation and his invention would likely be more practical around the beginning of the next century. We love our food too much and we don't need some upstart inventor telling us how to eat it or how to dump it.

Anyhow, I'm thinking about a better new way of dieting. I'll buy 35% less food and put rollers on the dining room chairs so they won't be so hard to push back.

**MRE - Meals Ready to Eat - usually for military personnel*

The Post Holiday Diet? Maybe 2014!

You know what you have to do now! You have to joyfully leap up and down and throw your whole body and soul into your New Year's DDD resolution. DDD stands for Disgustingly Depressing Diet. It is a fearful, daunting endeavor but you said you were going to do it come the New Year. Now we are almost a week deep in the New Year and you are still snacking at 2:00 AM.

Well, here we all are and I'm not sure if I possess deep resolve any longer and maybe I never did have deep resolve. The only thing deep about me is the distance from my belly button to my backbone and the deep stuff that appears around my feet when I'm not telling the truth.

I just read a long article in the news about how to get your diet jump-started and how to keep it rolling and how to persevere even though you are having sweet, drool-producing thoughts constantly haunting you. The article was so boring I fell asleep three times trying to read it. Another thing, there were so many dumb suggestions in the piece that to remember them all you either had to have perfect recall or three pages of instructions taped to your forehead. To tell the truth I did not read all of it. This electronic age is so wonderful. You can toss a nuisance story with just one little click. You don't have to wad and toss the paper and dispose of the trash later. With one little click you're free of all that nonsense.

How did you fare on your holiday hiatus of not watching your caloric intake? Was your caloric intake more like a food tsunami? I will admit that I am in pain from carrying an extra ten or twelve pounds around with me everywhere I go. I eat responsibly. I know I am responsible for eating everything on the table. There will be no waste. Remember what your Momma told you about all those little children starving in China? Well, don't worry yourself about all that. All those little Chinese children are fatter than we are. They are getting fatter too. The Chinese are getting rich from selling us gaudy dinnerware on which we pile heaps of food we cannot stop eating.

Maybe we can reflect further on this right before next Thanksgiving. If a fat attack doesn't take us far away, reflecting is probably all we are going to do because I can't imagine any Geezerdom residents losing much weight.

My reflections are on my pre-holiday diet. I was doing well until Thanksgiving rolled around. It was then that good Southwest Georgia friends shared with me an armload of quart bags full of shelled peanuts. They still had the skin on them and when Katie Mae fried a batch of them, and later, started roasting more of them in the oven, I ate peanuts twenty-four seven.

For breakfast I would have roasted peanuts and grits. Some mornings I would have roasted peanuts and yogurt. Then I tried roasted peanuts with cabbage but the best meal I had was roasted peanuts and collard greens cooked with neck bone. After the roasted peanuts and turkey and dressing my clothes began to shrink and I knew I was in trouble but I couldn't think of anything to do but eat some roasted peanuts and pumpkin pie. That was so good I tried roasted peanuts and ice cream on pecan pie.

The only thing I think I managed to do right was to sustain from drinking strong spirits. I did drink almost two bottles of beer with a meal one night at the Olive Garden but that was about it for me and boozing. In a weak moment I looked for a bottle of Georgia Moon that I had hidden. I keep having flashbacks of drinking it with old friends. A tiny flickering bit of memory makes me think I might have held a special prayer meeting over that bottle on New Year's Eve of 1960. I couldn't find it I think it's gone for good. Maybe that's why I remember so little about 1961.

Now back to dieting. All those diet gurus are now coming out of the woodwork and appearing on TV so they can get paid outlandish sums of money to tell us how to lose weight. Don't listen to them. They're young. Advice from young people like that could possibly kill us.

If we're still here by the time another new year rolls around let's discuss healthier eating habits and saner diets. It would probably be better to wait until about the middle of January (2014). We don't want to rush into a drastic diet program that could ruin our health instead of improving it. I promise to work hard at it but I honestly don't think I can get those peanuts out of my mind.

IV - MORE HEALTH ISSUES

Most of this is just for fun. The four-way bypass was not fun but you've got to know that we are the luckiest people alive. Nowhere in the world and at no other time in history have so many people been saved by medical advances like we have. My father died at 57 and I would have had the same fate at 59 if doctors had been unable to hook me up to a machine that breathed for me and pumped my blood through my body while the team took my heart and examined and worked on it like it was some old worn out Hacky Sack they were trying to rejuvenate.

They were successful and almost a dozen years later all I can say is, "Thank God they were good and am I a lucky guy?"

They Don't Serve Cabbage with a Four Way By-Pass!

When you near that sixtieth decade and you have worked double time to misspend your life, you have a much enhanced awareness of time. You know the Old Timekeeper can ring your chimes at any minute. This is my awakening story. This is when I thought I was hearing the bona fide pealing of the last bell.

I had lived in Southeast Georgia a couple of years when my heart started doing those little tap dance routines that leave you so breathless you have to flop down in a chair, take a huge gulp of air, get your lungs pumped up and pray your heart will go back to slow dancing. One afternoon I even drove over toward Swainsboro, Georgia from Stillmore, the little town where I worked, hoping to get a doctor to explain the soft shoe routines going on in my chest that made me gasp with fear and wonder. Strange erratic heartbeats would get my undivided attention in the mornings so, like a true idiot, I started out for the Swainsboro hospital one afternoon. It dawned on me that my heart only wanted to dance in the mornings. I turned around and went back to work. In the morning, two days later, my heart did an Irish jig and told me to go to the hospital in Swainsboro. I followed its advice. I signed myself into the emergency room.

If you live in a small town with a small town hospital, you know all about the trials and tribulations I encountered at the Swainsboro hospital. The personnel at this hospital were kind, gracious and caring folks. They are some of the world's nicest people. Unfortunately their facilities are terribly lacking in the multiple, strange needs of old guys like me and usually their brightest and best young people have left town and headed for the big city dollars. Fortunately there was a young emergency room doctor who was out of the Medical College of Georgia in Augusta and he worked the ER in Swainsboro part time. They immediately strapped me to an EKG machine and shot painless diagnostical electrical impulses through the muscle and flab tacked around my torso.

Then they snatched off the electrodes and what little chest hair I had, tossed my clothes back on me and the doctor, smiling professionally, said, "You've got what we call bigeminy. It's hard to track it because it is not occurring in a consistent pattern but you should have your cardiologist take a look at it. You have a problem there." Bigeminy, I learned was a pulse with two beats that are close together and then a pause followed by two more fast beats. My heart was doing the old fashioned two-step. I knew it had something to do with dancing. Naturally I let all worry take a back seat when the bigeminy went into a bashful, dormant state and did not dance in my heart again for a couple of months. The only follow up I had with the hospital was to allow them to strap a Holter Monitor to me with more dance music seeking electrodes taped all over me. I wore it for two days during which time I could not take a good bath. Not only did this screw up my love life for a couple of days but the hospital promptly lost the results from the Holter Monitor test. I never heard from them again. By now I had lost all seven of my chest hairs and what little dignity I possessed.

A few days later my Swainsboro doctor had an ultrasound technologist put cold gunk on my hairless chest and run an ice-cube cold wand all up and down my upper body, front and back, in an effort to ferret out the errant dancer inside me. It was so cold that my jaws locked and my cheeks were still purple thirty minutes later. Once again, test results were lost. I never received a report on the ultrasound until an alert, intelligent and persistent emergency room doctor at Phoebe Putney Hospital in Albany, Georgia retrieved them by phone from the Swainsboro doctor. He must have asked for the results more politely than I did but the test revealed no abnormalities.

Two weeks later, Katie Mae and I attended a Georgia Motor Trucking Association convention at beautiful Amelia Island, Florida and shortly after we arrived in Florida I discovered my old pal bigeminy had been in the car with us the whole time. Every time I thought I might have a little sip of an alcoholic beverage, the bigeminy bounce began. It is terribly disconcerting to have your heart dancing jigs when you are trying to do just the little things that normally get you through the day. The little things like walking, talking and steady, regular breathing.

As soon as the convention ended I told Katie Mae, "If I'm going to die, I'm going to die in Albany, Georgia with people I know and love around me and with medical care that makes me feel comfortable. We headed for Albany. Bigeminy was not invited but he came along anyway and he kept me company the entire trip.

I went straight to the Phoebe Putney Memorial Hospital emergency room. Good old Phoebe. She's gotten so big it's hard to see where she began and I don't think there will ever be an end to her. It is now a huge conglomerate spread all over the place in Southwest Georgia but you can bet your fanny you'll find the help you need in a larger town like Albany with doctors and facilities that can save you. However it was here at dear old Phoebe I almost fell through the cracks. This was only one of many close calls for a lucky boy who has always been under the clear-eyed scrutiny of a powerful Angel.

As I said the emergency room doctor obtained the ultrasound record from the Swainsboro doctor but it revealed little or nothing wrong with my heart. I was kept there a couple of days as they ran tests on me. The test they rely so heavily on is the nuclear stress test. At that point in my life, I had already had at least a dozen stress tests (over a span of about ten years) and the results always showed me to be in excellent shape. Once again, they slapped the tiny electrodes reinforced with duct tape on my tortured old torso. Then they stood me up on a treadmill. Keep in mind that this is not your standard, run-of-the-mill, for home-use-only treadmill. This bad boy will run up to forty miles per hour and they can jack it up to a 60 degree elevation so by the time you finish, you feel sure you have been running forty miles per hour up a hill somewhere on the steep side of the Rocky Mountains. They start you off just like you're walking on flat land at a leisurely pace. Usually you have four, three minute intervals of this misery. After the end of each three minute session, they increase the speed of the treadmill and they elevate it a little more. They only stop if you fall down or step on your tongue.

My slipping through the cracks was not the fault of the hospital or the doctors. My undoing was the fact that I have always done so well on a stress test. I could skip, leap, talk, sing and jump rope the whole time I was doing a stress test. I had three technicians in there with me. They assured me a person who could carry on like I was performing on the treadmill had little or no heart problems. Later, a doctor came by my room and assured me once again that I was in good shape. He said I had a little blockage in the arteries of my heart but I could effectively work on that with regular exercise and the Mediterranean Diet. They checked me out and I went home.

Three or four weeks later, Katie Mae and I came back to Albany. We still owned a house at my old home place and we were having repairs made to it so we could sell it. I was alone at the house for a couple of days doing some of the work myself. Bigeminy was no longer with me but when he left, he took all my energy with him. I noticed that I could only work for a few minutes before I had to sit down and rest. I also noticed that Katie Mae was making frequent visits by the house to check on me. She later told me I looked terrible and I was so lifeless and gray I looked the color of a serious rain cloud. I had a doctor's appointment in a couple of days. Katie Mae took charge and moved my appointment up to the very next day.

My doctor is a true lady. I think she is wonderful. When my old doctor retired, I asked specifically for a woman doctor. I had read that women actually listen to you and they are much more attentive than male doctors. I believed that then and I still believe it. The only problem is there are not enough female doctors out there and the ones practicing have no patient openings because they are so good.

I told her that I was in the emergency room only three or four weeks back and a member of her firm had told me I would be fine with an exercise program and the Mediterranean Diet and then I said, "Do you know what I think I am experiencing now?" When she answered, "What?" I said, "Classic heart attack symptoms." She responded with, "Oh my God, you are going straight upstairs to the cardiologist, right now!"

This is where you have just got to love a big old town and a big old hospital and a big old staff of people who can save your big old fanny in a pinch. Her office was in the hospital building. The cardiologist was only two floors up. They threw me on the elevator on the third floor and snatched me off the elevator on the fifth floor so fast I was still too dizzy to understand most of what the cardiologist told me when I arrived in his office. I do remember the word catheterization and I said, "When?" He said, "Right now!"

This was about five o'clock in the afternoon and I was by myself (meaning no loved ones were near). I said, "I am going to call my wife." When I got her on the phone, all I could say was, "You had better get up here. They're going to do something to me and I'm not sure what it is. I did hear him mention a gal named Cathy Rization and I don't know her but he spoke her name with such reverence she must do heart transplants!"

They shaved my groin and pumped me full of some of the best drugs you can imagine. There were two of them and we told jokes and lies while we waited on Katie Mae. When she arrived I gave her my most sincere "Good-bye" kiss and I started back on the joke telling routine until she tightened up on my collar which literally took my breath. At that point she said, "If you'll carefully notice, these two gentlemen have already scrubbed down and have their gloves on and they are holding their hands high in the air. They were just waiting on me to get here to kiss you goodbye before they begin to work on you so shut up and let them start!" Since I was doped to the gills and strapped to a gurney I gave in. I decided to let them start the show.

It gets really interesting at this point. It is especially intriguing if you are tied to a bed and there are a couple of guys beside you who are threading a miniscule tube through a freshly opened artery in your groin. How in the hell do they know how to get that miniature camera all the way from your lower abdomen to your heart without poking a hundred holes inside you? I should still know their names. Anybody who is messing around inside your body and taking tiny pictures of your heart, from the inside, should be your best friend and a lifelong buddy. How much closer can you get to another person? Of course Katie Mae has always held the strings to my heart in her delicate little hands but she has never actually poked around inside it and taken snapshots of it! I'm embarrassed. I don't even remember their names.

Amazingly I was not asleep. I continued to babble to these fine young gentlemen and they did a remarkable job of totally ignoring me. They had a twenty inch screen or monitor suspended from the nearest wall .The screen was over eight feet above the floor and we could all watch the action going on in my bewildered and foolish heart as they probed and clicked away with their pygmy camera. The moment of truth came to the bed-bound boy (that was me) when one of the fellows said, "There's your problem!" As I uncrossed my drunken eyes and finally focused on the monitor I could see the blood flowing freely through the vessels of my heart. I could see it going uphill and downhill and through passages to the sides but I could also see it reach a point where it stopped, dead cold! It looked like it had run into a stone wall. It just stopped. It is a chilling and eerie thing to see your own heart on a monitor while it is refusing to function like a good heart should.

This was 2001 and I was managing a truck line where one of our drivers recently had the same problem with his heart as I was now experiencing. The doctors in a Savannah hospital placed a couple of stints in his rebellious arteries and he was out of there and like brand new in two days. The same treatment was going on for Vice-President Dick Cheney who was up and on his way to helping save America in just a couple of days. I knew this was a simple fix so I told the guys, "Hey, I get a couple of stints and I'll be like new in a few days, right?" They stopped for a minute, sadly shook their heads and one of them said, "That ain't gonna work for you, podnah." I'm thinking, "Oh hell. We're starting to talk like cowboys." I instinctively knew we were about to cross Death Valley with no water and nothing wet around but my blood. John Wayne just warned me. It's all joking aside when John Wayne calls you "Podnah."

It was after five o'clock. One of the guys literally stopped what he was doing and left to catch the cardiologist before he left the hospital. He found him and brought him back to the room. The cardiologist took a look at the inside view of my heart and I was thinking how intimate this was getting. Three guys I just met are discussing things that are deep inside me. The doctor, not being that personable, looked sternly at me as if to say, "You have really screwed your heart up with all those years of eating chicken livers and washing them down with red liquor!" I felt like he knew everything about me by examining the innards of my pathetic heart but what he finally said was, "We are going to perform a bypass operation on you!" I said, "When?" He said, "The first thing in the morning!" Then he went out and talked to Katie Mae and told her they were going to do a three-way bypass the next morning. He told her I had 100% blockage in one artery and 90% in two other arteries.

I used to manage night clubs, juke joints and honkey tonks and normally I am not surprised or shocked by anything but I can confess to you that this floored me. Luckily I was in a drug-induced la la land and even more luckily, for me, they kept me slightly whacko through the entire ordeal. I have to rely on Katie Mae to tell me some of the things that happened to me because I stayed half knocked out the whole time. I have no idea why they operated on me so quickly. I have always thought that some unlucky soul was bumped from the operating schedule so they could work me in. I had been in no pain. I did not have a heart attack. I was simply breathless and had zero energy but I had no pain in my arms, jaw or chest. I did tell my doctor that a member of her firm had screwed up in their diagnosis of my condition and maybe that scared her into getting me fixed in a hurry. I never gave that much thought. I had never considered suing someone. My heart pumping along in a healthy condition appeals to me. Suing people does not appeal to me.

This was the first time I heard somebody mention cabbage. I was pretty freaked out at this point. The guys had already addressed me as "Podnah" and now I could hear the doctor talking about cabbage. Maybe he was having cabbage for supper. I love cabbage. I could eat a number three washtub full of steamed cabbage but soon I forgot all about greens for supper.

They put me in a cardiac care unit for safe keeping. They put a bag of sand (that's what it felt like) on my groin so the cut in the artery would clot properly. One neat thing they did was to give me some type of medication that kept me pretty well spaced out. This was especially helpful because I had no fearful thoughts through the night about a team of surgeons ripping up my chest with a Skill saw from Lowes. There was no cabbage served for supper.

In the morning they came for me. The orderlies were funny and we joked on the way down to the operating room. They made a stop so Katie Mae and I could kiss goodbye. They would not let her get on the gurney with me. I feared that would be my last disappointment.

I was pretty much in the dark for the next eight hours. I think I heard snips of several conversations that included something about cabbage. I was concerned that all these people were thinking only about their stomachs and not enough about my heart. The doctor looked like he was about twelve years old. For some reason, this didn't bother me. I felt like he was a brilliant young surgeon and that he would do a fine job patching my heart and as long as they continued to pump the good meds into my body, who cared?

The doctor had told us he was going to do a three-way bypass and he would harvest the needed veins from one of my arms and one from each leg. We choose the right arm because I'm a lefty. When we got in the operating room, he discovered he was going to be a vein short because it's going to have to be a four-way instead of a three-way so he harvested a vein from my chest. Even harvest, that word for collecting the veins, has such a sense of finality to it. You know the growing season is all over for the crop once it has been harvested.

They were very kind. They called Katie Mae from the operating room to tell her that my means of survival were now dependent on the proficiency of a heart-lung machine. I was now all hooked up to a machine that did my living for me while the doctors were playing catch and keep-away with an inanimate chunk of organ that has kept me in action for 59 years.

After working the miracles and wonders that these guys perform on a daily basis, the doctor again called Katie Mae to tell her my heart had all the cables and tubes reconnected and it fired up like the engine in a new Chevy Corvette. I was off the heart-lung machine and on my own again.

I was moved back to a recovery room where Katie Mae and our son Paul came in to see me. Paul was at the University of Georgia when he was told of my dilemma. He arrived after I was rolled into the operating room and this is the first time he has seen me in several months. He and Katie Mae were in a glum and depressed state of mind. They were staring down at me with such a forlorn look and with such sadness I felt like I had to do something to uplift the spirits of my little family so I slowly reached up, pulled the oxygen mask down on my chin and signaled with my forefinger for them to come closer. As they bent down and came nearer to my face, I sang to them in a croak that sounded like a bullfrog with laryngitis, "I love the night life, I got to boogie."

Paul was hysterical. People were staring at him and wondering why this crazy kid was laughing at the side of his freshly dissected Father. Kay was not so entertained. She bent closer and said, "There is a special ward here on the second floor where I can get you the serious help you need but they might not let you go home, you fruitcake!"

Recovery was great! I was there for a week. Many old friends and young and old relatives showed up. I had a small red pillow that was shaped like a heart and everyone autographed it. Sometimes I had to snatch it away from the signer when I had to laugh or cough. Laughing and coughing hurt like hell and the red pillow is still here at home somewhere. I hate to toss out such an old and dear friend. There is also a strange looking plastic contraption that I had to breathe into each day. It helped me rebuild and increase the strength and power in my lungs. It really hurt to breathe deeply. My chest had been split open right straight through the sternum and the two halves of my sternum spread wide enough for eight or ten people to do some ballroom dancing inside. When the doctors finished they then rewired the halves of my sternum together to keep the dancers out of there.

The physical therapy couple came by the very first day. I took a short walk with them. We made that short walk a bit longer each day. Toward the end of my stay I'm pretty sure that the nurses doubled up on my pain killer by accident. I was really snockered. I told Katie Mae that I thought they overdosed me. The physical therapy couple arrived but I was so drunk that I couldn't get out of bed. They were perplexed and confused. They kept saying, "But he was doing so well and now he can't walk!" They didn't understand "snockered." They finally left and the nurse came in to pull all those tubes from my chest and stomach.

I remember Lewis Grizzard's book "They Tore Out My Heart and Stomped That Sucker Flat" in which he described the horrible pain he suffered when they pulled the tubes out of him. I felt no pain. The nurses had inadvertently double-doped me. I'm pretty sure the tube-pulling nurse was so short she had to get up in the bed with me and put her foot on my chest so she could get enough leverage to snatch the tubes out of me: still, I felt no pain.

Something I did feel that will remain with me as long as I live is the bizarre sensation that occurred when the nurse pulled the wires from my heart. Two wires that ran from my heart to the outside of my chest were left there to jump start the heart in case it decided to take a break. When the nurse pulled those wires out, I could actually feel them unwind inside my chest. It felt to me like the wires had been wound inside my heart in the same fashion they wind the coil spring that retracts a push mower pull rope.

Before she left the room, I had to ask the nurse about the cabbage. "Where is the cabbage?" I queried. "What cabbage?" She replied. I told her how I kept hearing conversations all during my stay here about the cabbage but all I had seen on my plate since I had been here was red jello! "Where is the cabbage? I love cabbage. I could eat a ton of it. Do they ever serve cabbage around here or do they just talk a lot about it?" She seemed dumbstruck. She stared at me for a long time and then she said very slowly, "C-A-B-G is an acronym for Coronary Artery Bypass Graft and is referred to in medical terminology as Cabbage. You just had your cabbage, do you want some more?" I said, "Oh, no, no, no, I think I'll take a pass!"

After I was released we did not return to Swainsboro for a week. We stayed with Katie Mae's nephew, Ken, and his lovely wife, Kim. We love them as if they are our children and we stayed there with them as I recuperated. Their hospitality was never ending and we still owe our endless thanks and our undying gratitude to them. Their beautiful and intelligent young teenage daughter Kensley was only three years old at the time. She checked on the condition of my ravaged limbs every day and since I still had bloody scars from the knee to the ankle on each leg and from the elbow to the wrist on my right arm she was very concerned about my condition. One day she declared, "Your legs have crapped open!" I still think that was the best description I ever heard for the odd looking bloody crevices on my legs.

One morning everyone left for a memorial service for a much loved aunt who had just passed away. I sat there by myself in a big easy chair and watched the most unbelievable and horrible scene ever witnessed on live television as, not once but twice, airplanes commandeered by terroristic mad men flew into the twin towers of The World Trade Center.

I sat there for two more days and cried with thousands of other good Americans. I told Katie Mae to take me back to Swainsboro. I told her there was no way to get well when watching the incredible sadness created in the aftermath of this tragedy.

When we reached Swainsboro I called my young friend and co-worker, Tim Rich, and I told him I was not supposed to return to work or drive for a couple of weeks but I wanted him to pick me up each every morning and take me home at the end of each work day and that's what we did and that's how I recovered from my operation.

Eleven years later, a new cardiologist in Savannah says the bypass still looks good. I don't think about it much anymore. I don't think about cabbage much either. I do think about what matters most. I think about the people who died on September 11, 2001. I still think about them. I think about the people who killed our citizens that day. I think a lot about cultures and religions that support terrorism and approve the murder of people whose religious beliefs differ from their own beliefs.

For The Girls – Hot Flash Honeys and Menopause Madness

I understand that today's woman is going to spend more than one third of her life suffering menopause madness. I am also aware you women know all about proper diet and exercise and I sure as hell can't help you if you are suffering from vaginal dryness. First of all, I'm not familiar with that ailment because I don't have one and the few times in my sad life I was granted glorious and wondrous access to one, I became so embroiled in my own pathetic issues I forgot all about the poor gal's dire straits. It certainly was not an academic endeavor and here 55 years later I am still totally ignorant of the magical mechanisms that made it all so wonderfully possible.

Anyhow, I was reading this health magazine and I came across an article that insisted you can have a happy, healthy, harmless menopause. I wanted to share this article with all you geezerettes because I sincerely sympathize with those of you who are going through the menopause madness and I feel especially sorry for any poor guy who may be associated with you while you are suffering. I know you are inclined to make him hurt along with you if you are hurting. I like the "harmless" part the best because it means "Harm-Free" to me. I remember, all too vividly, a hasty retreat into a bathroom and slamming the door behind me in a flash but not soon enough to prevent a can of violently thrown hair spray from flying through a small crack left in the door just before it slammed shut. The hair spray can struck me with great force. It was the tall kind with 30% more spray in it, brand new, fully filled and heavy as hell. The can's bottom edge plowed a bloody furrow into my thinly skinned ankle bone. You know, it's the ankle bone that makes you cry when you slightly rake it on a door jamb or someone gives you a light lover's kick! The crying part is no joke. I was on the bathroom floor for over 30 minutes trying to assuage my flaming wound. I could hear evil cackles and laughs right outside the bathroom door. It was a horrible experience and I probably deserved some detention time for whatever it was that I had done but a hair spray can to the ankle is cruel and unusual punishment.

I feel proud that I can usually take my punishment like a man. Like the time I laid out drinking until the wee hours and came home in a drunken stupor and passed out in an empty bunk bed in my son's bedroom. I awoke the next morning to loud, screaming, blaring gospel music inside my tortured skull. I had an old transistor radio duct-taped to my head and it was tuned to the Sunday morning service from the Cutliff Grove Baptist Church. I never complained (much) about the radio or that removing the duct tape ripped half the hair from my head, but I admit, I'm still pretty pissed about the can to the ankle penalty.

So, in an effort to help you and my fellow (suffering) man out I wanted to pass on a couple of obvious things women can do if you have hit the age of the Hot Flash Honeys. Quit smoking. Smoking can kill you ten different ways and you have not given one single thought to any of those ways. Cutting out cigarettes can help your hot flashes. Don't drink too much booze or coffee and cut out spicy foods. Now I know you can do this because I have little will power and I have cut out booze and coffee and chocolate and most spicy food I only feel suicidal about every ten minutes so I know it can be done. I don't think I'm menopausal. I am old and worn out.

The ways to ease the menopausal pain and anguish are pretty obvious. What's less obvious is right there inside your head. Make time for yourself. Learn to relax as often as you can. Take breathers occasionally that help you air out your befuddled brain. It really helps to get the cobwebs out. Stop and watch yourself. Be more aware of your body and what you are doing with your hands and arms and legs and feet. Think about what you are doing. Think about the 'now moment.' What are you doing right now? Stop and think about the pen in your hand. Where did this copy paper originate? Was it produced from a tree in a huge rain forest far from here?

I just ate potato salad mixed with chicken salad and butter beans, all in the same bowl. I studied the food and the way it looked in the bowl and wondered why I put it all in the same bowl. I thought about my elbow. Contemplate your elbow. Relax. Did you know you can't kiss your elbow? Stop for a minute and try to kiss your elbow. Soon you will have everybody around you trying to kiss their own elbows. Life is tough. It can be less tough if you take time for yourself and your unkissable elbows.

Uncle Red Gets a Billy Goat Valve

Katie Mae is on the phone and I can hear the worry in her voice. The news is not good. Uncle Red is having medical problems and there are a couple of things that have the doctors perplexed. First of all he had a nasty fall that left him with a slight bleed in his brain. This has to be taken care of before they can tackle the major problem which they discovered only after they had stabilized his dizziness from the fall. After taking a stress test Uncle Red was found to have a heart valve that had calcified like a piece of petrified wood and if they couldn't get that valve replaced, soon, Uncle Red was not going to have a bright future.

The first thing the family heard was Uncle Red's heart valve was going to be constructed from a pig's tail. His daughter Sissy had tearfully related this sad news to Katie Mae on the phone. I had a four way by-pass back in 2001 so I understand more than a little about coronary artery bypasses and I know they have used pig valves to replace human heart valves but who in the hell ever heard of replacing a heart valve with tissue from the pig's curly tail? The whole family was in a tizzy. Red and his brood are all out in Louisiana and I know those Cajuns and Coon Asses do things a little differently out there but a heart valve from a pig tail was more than I could handle. Maybe Red's doctors were on one of those reality shows out there. In that case, I would have understood it if they wanted to replace Red's valve with something off an alligator or a possum but using a pig tail was awfully hard to imagine. They even had me picturing the doctors cutting out a little round section of the pig tail and shaping it into a little round heart valve. That was shortly before I looked in the mirror and slapped myself back into the right frame of mind.

I knew Red was feeling low because of his condition and especially because old Red liked to smoke a cigarette and drink a cold beer on occasion and, as you know, neither one is allowed for a guy as sick as he was; he was practically a prisoner in that big hospital. So it was, "No smokes and no brew" for Red. I knew he was scared and lonely and pretty unhappy there so I thought I might cheer him up a little bit if I gave him a call. I'm from South Georgia and I talk slow like a lot of people from the South but my first real job was working with a bunch of mean-ass Irish guys from Metuchen, New Jersey and the first thing I learned from them was how to out-talk them. I can pick my speech patterns up about ten or twelve notches and talk just like a mean-ass New Jersey Irishman.

So I did that and when Red answered the phone I immediately went into a long spiel about my name was Frank Murphy and I was an associate of his doctors. I told him I had been assigned to locate the proper tissue to be used in the heart valve replacement and unfortunately we had not been able to locate the correct porcine or pig valve and we had the same bad luck in finding bovine or tissue from a cow that we could use. I then said, "We were extremely lucky to locate some tissue from a kid, and by kid, I do not mean a small child, but rather we have a perfect match by using the ass-hole of a baby billy goat!"

I could hear gasping and coughing on the other end of the line and it scared the hell out of me. I was praying, "What if I have killed him! Dear Lord, please don't let him die."

I threw the phone at Katie Mae and said, "Try to talk to him I think he may be dying!" She held the phone for a few seconds and looked at me and said, "No, you fool. He's laughing!"

I was scared to death. I refused to talk to him again. As it turned out the operation was a great success. They used the bovine tissue. Hooray for Red. He made the cut!

He's out and about now and even though he's a free man, he has not felt the need for beer or cigarettes. I was not sure which animal tissue they used until Sissy called a few days ago and said that everything was great with her Daddy except every time they drive pass a Chick-Fil-A billboard he starts mooing in a low voice.

Rusty Bottoms and the Taint Tonic

Rusty Bottoms had a problem. Rusty had a pain he thought was being produced by his prostate gland. He visited his general practitioner who was a little bit puzzled by poor Rusty's unknown malady and the doctor did not provide anything in the way of good medical advice that helped him. The only relief resulting from the visit was the relief the doctor felt when he saw Rusty paying the lady at the checkout desk.

Rusty asked my advice and I told him to see his urologist. Rusty said he was afraid of pain and didn't want a stranger poking him in that most private (for a man) of orifices. I said, "Rusty, you are a wimp and a wuss. We are talking about prostate cancer prevention here, and if little old gals with virtually no breasts can let somebody perform a major boobie bashing mammogram on them checking for breast cancer, you can at least man up long enough to take a posterior prodding." I mentioned small-breasted women because I understand they don't have large enough breasts to get them completely between those vise-like plexiglass pressure plates. A technician has to throw a body block and then bulldoze them from behind in order to get enough boob in the vise to test.

I also told old Rusty that a PSA test is good but not always perfect and if the results from a PSA are questionable, you should have a digital exam, often fondly referred to as a "finger wave," because the urologist can feel at least one side of the prostate during the digital exam and if he feels nodules (which is not a good sign) on that one side at least you can have a head start on trying to clear things up before they go too far.

So Rusty goes to the urologist and things work out well for him. He has a great PSA number and the urologist detected no abnormalities in his prostate during the rectal exam. This is about where things began to go downhill for Rusty Bottoms.

Rusty tells the doctor that he has a terrific pain occurring in the area of his "taint" when he does yard work or anything too strenuous on his back. The urologist is from New York and he gives Rusty one of those wide-eyed, slack-jawed quizzical looks and says "Taint?" Rusty says, "Yeah, my taint. You know where the taint is, don't you? You studied medicine all that time and they never told you about the taint?" So the doctor says, "Hell no. Just where the hell is the taint and why do they call it that?"

And sure enough Rusty tells him, "It's right between my sack and my rectum and they have always called it that because on a woman, it taint a-hole and it taint p***y. It's just taint." I had to stop Rusty right there and ask, "Good God man, you didn't say that to the doctor did you? You didn't use the words a-hole and p***y in a serious conversation with a doctor about your medical condition?"

"I damned sure did", said Rusty and you know what he did? He sat down and wrote me a prescription for some ointment to put on my taint. He told me it's 94% compounding salve and 6% Gabapentin. Gabapentin is the generic name for Neurontin and it's is used by epileptics and even has an off-prescription use for people like diabetics who have nerve damage to their hands and feet. You know, like the damage I've got. It's called peripheral neuropathy. I'm not diabetic but I sure as hell have PN. They have learned it can be used on your taint for pain and the only difference is that epileptics and diabetics take it orally and I use it in an ointment form. I Googled this stuff and gynecologists are using it on women who have had severe pain or injuries to their vaginal area. It does something to calm injured nerves. I tell you the damned stuff works and I'll tell you what else the doctor told me as he was leaving the room." He said, "Thanks for the demotics." "I thought he said, "Thanks for the demonics." I believed he thought I was some kind of devil worshiper or demon or something but I went and Googled that too and demotics are just a common way of saying something. He must think I'm real common, like dirt."

The story gets worse. Rusty had his prescription filled by one of these pharmacists who compound things and the resulting tab was sixty-five bucks. Rusty is fairly bright and since he already had a super-sized bottle of Gabapentin capsules he used for his nerve damage in his hands and feet he decided he could make his own taint tonic. He found a pair of fairly accurate scales in his pantry that were supposed to be used for weighing food portions when you're on a diet. Then he took about 50 of the Gabapentine pills and a jar of Vanicream that women use to moisturize their skin and he broke open each of the pills and mixed the contents of the pills with the Vanicream. He used the same amount of Vanicream that was needed to fill the little dispenser bottle he got from the pharmacist. Rusty's ointment mix cost him $4.38. He was now off and running on the taint, self-treatment gig of his life.

About three weeks later Rusty calls me and said, "I've got a real problem." I said, "What's wrong with you?" Rusty says, "They're blue." I said, what's blue?" and he said, "My testicles are blue." By now I'm shouting, "You've got blue balls?" Rusty is moaning and groaning, "Yeah, yeah, yeah, what can I do?"

I hated to do this but I had to tell him, "Quit dating that extremely chaste woman you've been going with. Go find your old girlfriend, the one we used to call Loose Lucy, and for God's sake, quit making your own taint tonic!"

Old Goats

As I have grown old and continue to grow older (thank God), I am fascinated by people who are even older than I am and how they have managed to hang in there for so many years. Do they have secrets we can pry out of them that will help us win the gold in longevity?

The object of my latest fascination is none other than Charles (Ches) McCartney, better known as America's Goat Man. McCartney was born in 1901 (maybe) and he died in 1998 (for sure). He would have been 97 at the time of his death but no one knows exactly when he was born. He may have been over 100 when he died. Let me throw out a few strange facts and dumb questions about the lifestyle of America's Goat Man and you tell me if his lifestyle had anything to do with how long he lived. Ches left home (Sigourney, Iowa) when he was about fourteen and ran away to New York City.

My question is: Did running away from home increase his life span? No more of that "Bring in the dog and put out the cat!" type Yakety Yak from his home folks.

He married a 24 year old Spanish knife thrower. She learned there was more money to be made in exhibitions at bars and diners if she used Ches as a target instead of her usual dart board. He learned if he kept her knife points sharp, she would make the knife stick in the backstop on the first throw.

That way she didn't have to throw the same knife twice because it failed to stick in the board the first time.

Many questions come to mind:

How long was he married to her before he became her main target? Did he understand that becoming her target was non-habit forming? How long did it take him to learn a sharp knife sticks and holds better than a dull knife (in wood and flesh)? Do stupid people live longer?

The knife slinger became pregnant so Ches took her back to Iowa to the farm. A tree fell on him and he was so badly injured, people thought he was dead. He was revived by an undertaker prodding and poking him. Question: Will a near death experience inspire you to live longer.

The great depression slam-dunked his farming, and his cash flow. He was cleaned out, even out of his old worn out over-alls. He had a few goats left over from his farming venture. He got his wife to construct neat and fashionable outfits from goatskins for him, herself and their small boy child. He built two totally rickety, ramshackle, iron-wheeled, wagon-like vehicles. He piled his wife and the boy and his few worldly possessions in the wagons and hit the road. She soon bailed out on him and the boy and for 38 years he took this crazy caravan up and down the roads of America. He sold pictures and post cards of himself, the wild wagons and the goats. The wagons were covered in lanterns, pots and pans, wash tubs, pails and buckets, old auto tags and other scraps of metal. He lived on hand-out meals and goats' milk and what little food he bought when he bought hay for the goats. He claimed he was an ordained minister and would preach sermons. He could curse blue streaks just as well as he could preach if he happened to injure himself. He claimed to have traveled over 100,000 miles. He often said the Lord had promised seven wives for every man and he had married three and left the other four for some other lucky man to snag. He was not known for being truthful.

Questions – Will traveling with goats at one MPH and listening to a small child and a woman talking 90 MPH when you are walking one MPH make you a little bit wary of spending your whole life with other people, especially women who tend to ask a lot of questions that you cannot answer and the 32 goats must have been raising a hell of a racket too? If the woman divorces you and you send the boy home to live with your parents, can you tack a few more years onto your time line?

McCartney would go for years without bathing. He said the goats did not care how he looked or smelled. The more layers of dirt he had on him, the warmer he was in cold weather and if the temperature got down to 30 degrees, he would drag a goat in the wagon with him for additional warmth. If it got down to zero, he said, "That was a five goat night."

There are a lot of questions I have about the connection between how he lived and how long he lived.

If you look like a goat and smell like a goat and few people come near you and those who do, don't linger long in your odoriferous presence and if you have little or no contact with women who talk an awful lot about many different subjects that are abstract, oblique and of little significance and you are encapsulated in several layers of bacteria-defying dirt and you drink goat milk all day long and you walk from six to ten miles every other day are you capable of living longer than 99.99% of all the people who have ever inhabited the earth.

I leave it to you who read this to decide if you want to give it a try. As for me, I'm a creature of comfort and there is little doubt in my mind that the good Lord meant for me to carry on with my foolishness in air conditioned dwellings.

Birthday Potpourri Chuckeletto

Tuesday November 6, 2012. Today is election day. Today is my birthday.

The fun began Friday before my birthday. Ken, Kimberly and Kensley came from Albany in Southwest Georgia. Katie Mae's sister Sharon came from Summerville-near-Charleston. Paul was already here. The house was nearly full. Everybody talked at one time. Sharon brought enough food to feed many people for many days. She brought exotic salads and cheeses and those Crunchmaster crackers that I would kill for. Katie Mae made a large pot of chili and another big pot of a special Lima bean soup that she likes to make for Ken.

Kimberly brought a pound cake to me for my birthday. Hope White baked it and it is so good that I did not want to share it. I fantasized about hiding in the closet and eating it all by myself. Ken and I (and everybody else) were especially fond of the crunchy crust that ringed the cake at the bottom. I went ahead and shared it in spite of my greed. I wondered if Hope White's husband has the same problem I do. Katie Mae is a fantastic cook and I have a lard tire that waxes and wanes around my waist like the rings around Saturn. Luckily for me, Katie Mae is not a cake-baking, pie-making enthusiast as well as a super cook or I would have long ago gone the way of all fat boys with too many clogged arteries.

On Saturday morning we went to the UGA/Ole Miss game. We saw old friends. We enjoyed the largesse of Britt and Andrea and all the others who contributed food and drink for the benefit of the masses at SwilleyGate. I reported the game on http://www.geezergrit.com under the title "Athens-UGA-Homecoming 2012."

We stayed at the game for hours and by the time the youngsters dragged the oldster home, I was suitable for framing...by my headboard, foot board and my bed covers. They kept referring to me as, "The Old Waddler." I cannot multitask. I cannot eat and drink that much and walk straight. I should have demanded a wheel chair.

Sunday came and I actually got out of bed pretty early and stood almost straight up! The youngsters were scattered but I rounded them up and watched their eyes shine as I explained the attraction of a deep gulley not too far down the road from our house. I told them about all the gold that has been found in Georgia and how, no doubt in my mind, that gold can be found at the bottom of that gulley in certain spots. I neglected to tell them the gold was discovered further north in the Georgia mountains but it really didn't matter. They left with a small shovel, a bucket for soil samples and their eyes all aglitter.

They returned with just the bottom of the small sample bucket covered in mud. I was thinking this is a pretty meager sample but these are city kids and I better not try to work them too hard. They may fall out on me and there is just no way I'm going to be able to pick any of them up. I couldn't even get Ken Ken back to the house in a wheel barrow and she's the lightest one of the lot. I take the sample bucket and tell them we will pan that mud and get the results later. I thought if there was any gold in it, I might have to check it out for purity and negotiate ownership later on.

Then they got a couple of plastic grocery bags and start raking acorns from beneath this huge white oak tree in the front yard. This is referred to as "mast" by my woodsy friends in South Georgia. If you follow my drift, you know what I mean and if you are a woodsy guy from the south, you know what the mast is for. We spread it out in a perfect place behind my house. Now we will have furry friends as well as feathered friends although I am not too sure birds and animals think of us as friends, or think of us at all. It reminds me of the lady bitten by the monkey who couldn't understand why the monkey bit her. She knew the monkey liked her because he always grinned at her. She was a little slow on the uptake. When the monkey grins at you, it is a warning he does not like you and to get the hell away from him before he bites you.

Sharon left early, Ken, Kimberly and Kensley left a few hours later and we shared a big pizza with Paul for dinner.

The weekend was over and the birth/election day was on the way. When it all hit, the election results were not what I hoped for but the birthday was good because I am still alive and I enjoyed it for the humorous moments it gave me. That's why I called this Birthday Potpourri Chuckeletto. I know you don't quite spell chuckle the way I have it but my way works better for me. It is a small mishmash of chuckles I encountered on my birthday. I'm sharing them with you because I think we need something like a good chuckle several times daily to get us through the day and help balance the happiness with the sorrow we encounter. I hope these help you, even if only for a little while.

Katie Mae's birthday card to me reads: "In life you're either the HAMMER or the NAIL...so on your BIRTHDAY, the question becomes .... (open the card and it says) "Would you rather get hammered or nailed?"

Now she asks me! Would I rather get hammered or nailed and I'm too damned old to do either. The health gurus have seen to that. At least the thought was kindhearted and I accept all invitations with an open mind. The spirit is willing but, unfortunately, the spirit is out there free-wheeling in space. Isn't that what they say? The spirit is willing and you know the rest about the weakness of the flesh. Damn, I'm foiled again, by a feeble mind and a misspent youth.

"If a frog keeps his mouth open too long, he will suffocate." This was on a birthday card I received. Why would someone buy a card like this? What did I do to deserve this card? Is it true? Did some strange person watch a frog hold his mouth open too long and then offer him absolutely no help when he began to suffocate. He could have been given mouth to mouth. I'll bet those science labs have little bitty paddles you can use to jump start a frog's heart. Did someone in one of those chambers of horror in medical school use tiny dental clamps to hold the frog's mouth open until he choked down his last breath? Was the frog green? Did his face turn blue or purple? We need serious answers to serious questions asked here. I want to know if there are people going around deliberately suffocating frogs. I love Kermit. Is he safe? I want answers; I just don't know who to ask.

Another birthday card declared that after you reach fifty, Happy Birthday becomes an oxymoron and the sound of someone saying, "Happy Birthday," brings thoughts of fingernails scraping on a black board. It is the lower frequencies of the nails scraping that drives us mad. Scientists tell us it is comparable to a primitive warning cry of certain monkeys. Monkeys and primal thoughts keep troubling me. After all these fleeting eons have flashed by us we still have those fearful scream receptors fused into our brain cells. In our fight or flight response to this cry, we most naturally try to run from the encroaching frailties of old age. It almost makes sense….. to a monkey. This was a hand-made card from an old friend who is institutionalized. Don't worry. I don't think they'll ever let him out.

The last weird card I received was from my elderly son out in Texas. He is about twelve years older than I am and I think I got my twisted sense of humor from him. Anyhow, the card was okay and suitably funny but he chose to enclose a note from retired attorney, Frank Faulk, Sr. The note is a verbatim copy of a letter sent to the claim agent's office of the A&Y

Railroad in Greensboro, NC. The author of the letter was dead serious.

Mr.Faulkner
A&Y Railroad
Greensboro, NC

Your railroads rund over my bul at the 20 mile pass on Wensday. He air not ded, but he mout as well be and I want your sexion boss repote him ded and pade for. He mash out both his seeds leafing mity little of his bag hit tared out a peace of skin a foot squar betwixt his pecker and nabul, he air totaly unqualifide to be a bul and he air mamed up to bad to be a steer and he air to dam tuf for beef, so I want you to repote him ded and pade for and so fofe.

P.S. He were a red bul, but he stands around looking mity blew these days.

It kind of makes me proud that I am 71 and I have never had problems like that. Birthdays are wonderful aren't they? Just keep those chalk-board monkey-screams to a minimum and don't trust a live monkey if he grins at you.

Looking Back

Do you ever stop to reflect on some of the crazy things you did when you were young that are now making you wince and moan and grumble with the stress of trying to do something simple like get out of bed in the morning or bend over to put on your socks? If you are as screwed up as I am, you do not bend over to put on your socks. You have to sit on a little bench or stool and gently coax your socks over your toes with one hand at a time as you attempt to bend just slightly forward toward your feet. If you can do this and cuss at the same time, you have not lost your ability to multi-task. We have lived our youth during the best years Americans have ever seen and one thing youngsters have on us today is they are more educated about stress on the back and spine and what permanent damage stress can do to a person's back and joints. They also have labor-saving devices that can help them pick up and move large objects that we used to have to move manually. Probably the thing that is really saving their backs is that most of them are lazy as hell and they are not going to pick up anything heavier than a knife and a fork (they don't need spoons because we are still spoon feeding them).

The reason I brought this up; my back is killing me. I feel like an old broke-back mule. I was told about 50 years ago by an orthopedist that I have scoliosis which is a lateral curvature of the spine. The spine has a natural front to back curvature but the lateral curvature is abnormal. I forgot all about scoliosis until about five or six years ago when my back pain began to gradually increase. I knew I had degenerative vertebrae, which generally makes you have screaming fits, and I expected aging would not improve the degenerative part. Aging seems to cause further degeneration. Can you believe it? Nothing seems to get better at 70.

I went to my general practitioner who sent me to one of those groups who have pleasant looking women who are not really pleasant. Most of them are descendants of people who designed Nazi torture machines. I was not sure where the name "Physical Therapy" came from or what it meant until I had a visit each week for several weeks with some of these unbelievably happy women. They joyfully punch and poke at you and twist you with great glee and hum pleasant little tunes as they try to rip limbs from time worn sockets. Now I know what "PT" stands for. It is an oxymoron that means "Pleasant Torture."

One day when the crippling bitch from Buchenwald, who was torturing me, showed a human side to the beast in her and went off to the rest room, I crawled away from there as fast as I could. I found solace in knowing that I was still alive which made me feel much better physically for about two years and then the pain began to ratchet up on me again.

I arranged an appointment with a pain management professional who immediately told me that he managed pain, not with oral medications, but with a computer guided hypodermic needle straight into the spine. I want you to understand that he was talking about my back and my spine and I felt a dirty crawling sensation run up and down that very same spine and something in me recognized him as just one more merchant of torture.

I might have been fortunate in my decision to by-pass the shot of steroids to the spine since I follow the national news as much as possible and it has been a pretty bad situation for a large number of people who have been taking the shots which were manufactured in a lab in Massachusetts. Hundreds of people have grown ill from the contaminated steroids in the vaccines and over forty people are dead from the tainted shots.

I declined his invitation to shoot me up in the spinal cord and as I was leaving he recommended the physical therapy office across the hallway and, even though I knew better, I went through the door right into the arms of another "mad-at-the-world" mean woman just thrilled for the opportunity to see me scream and cry real tears. Boy was I surprised to find that this gal was actually a human being with a big heart and not the heartless robot I had envisioned.

She made me take my shirt off and told me to turn around so she could look at my spine. After she took a good look, she said, "Do you know you have scoliosis?" Believe it or not, I had forgotten all about the scoliosis. It had been about 45 years since the old home town orthopedist had told me I had it and it never seemed to bother me or cause me any problems. Not being the brightest light on the chandelier I mumbled, "Is that causing me a problem?" She said, "Well it throws your spine all out of whack and causes a lot of the pain you are experiencing and the worst part about it for you and your spine is one of your legs is shorter than the other."

"Really, I said, which one is the shortest?" She told me my left leg was shorter. I put my shirt on, thanked her and rushed right on down to Wal-Mart where I located a whole aisle of heel supports and arch supports and whatever else I could find to put in that left shoe so my legs would be the same length or, at least, closer to the same length.

For over five years those heel supports kept me virtually pain free and I am sharing this with you in hopes you can also take a closer look at what doctors are telling you and at the many different ways you can possibly help yourself avoid pain and ailments. There is a world of good doctors in this country but being good creates a problem after they have been practicing a few years. A good doctor gets covered up with too many patients and he begins to have less and less time he can spend with you on each visit.

Always see your doctor but remember nobody knows your body like you do and if there are ways to avoid sickness and pain that work for you don't be afraid to entertain those methods. Tell your doctor what you're doing. If he has no problem with it, give it a shot.

Slow Down, You Move Too Fast

If you are an up and coming boomer, you might have noticed you are not as sure of foot as you once were. Start looking for ways to improve your stability and balance. If everything fails, start looking for walls and chairs and most any inanimate object you can prop on or use for support. Other people can be pretty good props if they are not as feeble and shaky as you are.

If you drop something, don't try to catch it unless it is extremely valuable and fragile. Trying to catch an object you have dropped can be very risky. If it is a knife, let it go and try to get your feet out of the way without falling over. I once caught a steel rod that was pointed on one end by just using the palm of my hand. That was 55 years ago and I can still see the scar.

In illustration:

Our old friend, Bubba Jack Johnson was still living at home when he was 65. Bubba's Mama was a large woman we called Mama Jack. Mama Jack stood about six and a half feet tall and weighed just a shade over 400 pounds. I never knew Papa Jack. I understand that he was fairly small in stature and actually slept in the same bed as Mama Jack until they found him in a breathless state one morning. Mama Jack's pounding on his chest in her attempts to jump start his heart, cut his chance of survival from slim to none. Death was attributed to COPD and I guess that's a good description as any for what happens to you when a six foot, six inch, 400 pound woman falls into a deep sleep and rolls over on top of you.

Anyhow, Bubba was taking a shower one morning in the master bathroom. He liked showering there because it was roomy and it had a built-in bench where you could sit if you got tired. While he was washing behind his sizable ears, he dropped the wash cloth. It slipped down the front of his chest and headed south for the shower floor. In his haste to retrieve the wash cloth, Bubba Jack threw his right hand down, grabbed for the cloth, got a hand full and snatched his hand back up with great force.

Unfortunately Bubba had grabbed a hand full of curly hair that grew so profusely around that area down there that is known as the nether region. When he snatched his hand back up, not only did he scalp his groin but his ass came with the hair and he threw his ass completely over his left shoulder. EMT's and firemen had to use two hydraulic jacks to pop his fanny back into place. A team of hair transplant surgeons reattached his pubic hair and it took four nurses to remove all those splinters from his buttocks that came from the boat paddle Mama Jack used to beat him with when she saw that torn up shower stall.

Just watch out for what you go grabbing in a hurry. It can get you in a lot of trouble.

Your Shoes and Your Gimpy Feet Blues

Your feet are killing you because we always made a special effort to buy, beg, borrow or steal the worse shoes that ever shod flat feet. If you are still wearing flip-flops, dock shoes and other flats with no arch support, your feet are so flat by now that you are walking two inches below street level. There were absolutely no arch supports to be found in the shoes we used to wear. You couldn't have found a single pair of arch supports in a thousand pairs of those super cool loafers and dock shoes we wore.

And don't forget all that fat you have picked up in the last forty years. If you got that much bigger, did it ever occur to you that your feet got fatter too. You are probably walking around in shoes a size too small with soles as flat as fritters. When you take your shoes off and you see all those deep lines and impressions running across the top and down the sides of your feet, do not become alarmed about having congestive heart failure (unless you have congestive heart failure). Your shoes are too little for you. Stop being such a masochistic old goat and go get your feet checked out. Get some shoes that fit you and get some that have arch supports! See if you can coax some arches back into those flat tires you keep referring to as feet.

If you are an early stage boomer hitting your sixties and if you are still running or jogging, and your feet hurt you to the point that you can hear them screaming don't cuss them and don't talk back to them. Evaluate what you are doing to them. Your feet are old. Walking places a lot of stress on certain parts of the foot and running exerts three times that pressure. You are jogging down that long lonely road to Geezerville and you want to hang on to your feet. It will not be fun for you if you outlive your feet. You know the people I'm thinking about. They are the less fortunate of us who are saddled to canes, crutches, walkers and wheelchairs.

I want to curse my feet every day but my feet are blameless. I am the dummy who, as a kid, wore dumb shoes that caused a great deal of the pain I now suffer. My only salvation was finding better shoes and making enough money to pay for better shoes before I lost total use of my feet. I found Rockport and Reebok and eventually Reebok bought Rockport and eventually Adidas bought Reebock so now I don't know who owns what and I feel sure almost all our shoes are made in China but I do know that the DMX construction used in many of the Rockport and Reebok shoes are the most comfortable I have found for my feet. They also have a wider shoe now for people like me with feet that geezered up and got fatter. These shoes cost more but they are worth it and they usually last and last.

If you are a clumsy klutz like me you should stay away from shoes with Velcro flaps and tabs. Velcro tie-downs have a diabolical way of loosening as you shuffle along. The inside of your right foot can rub the inside of your left foot as you walk. A flap on one foot will playfully jump out and bind itself to a flap on the other foot and they will become attached to each other just like you put them together with super glue. Your shoes begin to move as one (with your feet in them). You will think you have gone back to playing hopscotch with the girls in the third grade. This will occur to you only a mini-second before you root up about a yard of pavement with your nose.

Be careful with your feet and where you put your feet when you walk.

Toenails

Over fifty years ago Coach Graham Lowe and Coach Bob Fowler taught us in the seventh grade to use big toenail clippers that clip your nails straight across so you won't have ingrown nails. We were unsophisticated country boys and some of our guys were using knives, machetes and weed eaters (with the lawn-edging attachment) to keep their nails from getting too ragged. Back then some people kept going to school forever. We had people in high school well over twenty years old with beards so thick they should have shaved twice a day. Their toenails were lethal weapons. We started cutting our toenails straight across so we would not develop the dreaded ingrown toenail.

My old buddy C. Tross has his own devilish method. He has been cutting his toenails for years using what I call the vampire pattern. He uses a secretive and tortuous tool that leaves his toenails in a wicked "V" shape. The ends or sides of the nails jut out like daggers and the centers have artistic indentations. His wife has serious scarring on her lower legs and spends her evenings sleeping on the couch. If you are still sleeping with that wonderful woman you married, but you feel like you need more snooze room for yourself, use the C. Tross system of nail trimming to gain a greater share of the bed at night, or the whole bed for that matter.

After going to a lot of trouble cutting my toenails straight across for over thirty years it occurred to me that I have never had an ingrown toenail. Now that I am a worn out old coot and still cutting my own toenails I find that I can barely touch my toes even sitting on a little stool about a foot off the floor. I can barely reach my feet to trim my nails so I decided to cut them like I cut my fingernails and not worry about it. That was twenty years ago and I have not had an ingrown toenail in all that time.

You might not want to try anything different with your feet but it does make you wonder why you do the things you do. Was it something you read; something you saw on television repeated by someone, who probably is not as bright as you are, or did Coach Lowe and Coach Fowler tell you to do it in the seventh grade?

As I said, you probably don't want to try this, especially if you are diabetic. You could start with a sore toe and wind up losing your whole foot. If you still have all the walking gear God gave you at birth, and you are still ambulatory, a foot is definitely something you want to hold on to.

Recently I noticed my toenails had taken on new life of their own. I thought I was suffering from some kind of, "Old

Man's Toenail" or I'm going through a toenail rebellion. The nails on two or three toes had begun to thicken and the sides curved downward to the point I was having trouble cutting them. I seriously thought that this was a byproduct of aging and I had nothing to worry about. It did concern me a little because I began to think little fingers were growing from beneath my toenails. Katie Mae said I was being stupid. I remember trying to let the nail on a big toe grow as long as I could when I was a kid. I wanted the nail to curve under the toe and just keep on growing back under my foot. I was going to bill myself as, "The Teenaged Toenail" and charge the other kids for taking a look at it. It didn't work. The darned thing kept breaking off.

This new malady, I soon learned from a good doctor is a fungus. He said he could get me a prescription that would clear up my nails but it would cost $800.00 and that my case really wasn't that serious. I told him I thought it was pretty serious if it cost $800.00 to clear it up. I went home and checked on home remedies. I tried Vick's Vaporub on my toenails for about a bottle and a half's worth and decided that probably was not working. I put my nails to the "Toenail trimming test" and they were just as hard to trim as they were before. My toenails were the same but my sinuses had become so clear I could see for forty miles. I had our house smelling like Henry Crawford Tucker's place when twenty of his thirty-two children caught a cold.

Then, upon Katie Mae's sage advice, I tried another old home remedy and began to soak my nails in Listerine. This seems to have worked to some degree because the little fingers growing from beneath my nails were becoming softer and you could make them wiggle if you pinched them and shook your foot at the same time. The toenail trimming test is coming up soon for the Listerine treatment and I will let you know how that has turned out.

Meanwhile, Katie Mae has found me a new cure that I have not tried as of yet. It called "Miracle Anti-Fungal Treatment" and it is distributed by Ontel Products Corp. and there is a little blurb at the top of the box that is totally reassuring because it reads, "As Seen on TV." I feel better about it already. The "Before Toe" pictured on the box is gross and funky looking with scaly skin and a toenail so discolored it looks like the putrid yellow inside a bad tomato. My toes do not look like this at all. I do not have itchy, scaly skin and I don't think my toes smell bad because Katie Mae would have me sleeping in the basement if I had smelly feet. I do not think this is the kind of fungus I have but I'll soon let you know how those little fingers living under my toenails are doing after I have tried this for a month or so. I would be some kind of upset if I lost all my toes. They are ugly but I really like them right there on the ends of my feet.

After I first wrote this I decided the fungus medicine Katie Mae purchased for me was actually for athlete's feet. I do not have athlete's feet so I quit using it but I did go back and use a whole large-sized bottle of Listerine on my toenails over about a three or four month period. I applied it sparingly each morning. I dabbed it on with a q-tip. I think it might have helped because the nails became softer and cleaner and whiter looking. They were easier to cut and I felt so good about them, I danced shoeless in a downtown Athens restaurant. I'm proud of my toes and nails. They look like I bleached them. I'm thinking about painting the toenails black. That'll look good on my bleached out white toes.

Go see a podiatrist if you can manage it. Let the doctor look at your ugly feet (there are no pretty feet after you get past sixty) and give you an opinion on whether, "Yo feets are failing you now!"

Falling Out With the Gout and the Pain of PN

I started talking about feet because you have to start somewhere and our feet were our first means of motivation. Our feet put us out on the road right up to where we are now. We will eventually work our way up to the head. We'll talk about it later because the head won't be as interesting since most geezers have empty heads.

Gout – There are no known atheists who have suffered the gout. Gout will make true believers of the world's worst heathens. Deep in your body there is a demon who waits patiently until, one evening, you come home, you have a shooter or two before dinner and then you pig out on a delicious sirloin steak and wash down all that red meat with good red wine or a beer or two and later, just when you get settled into that peaceful, restful sleep you are so looking forward to, there comes a little twinge or twist in your big toe. You don't know it yet but a demon has you by that toe and before the next two or three days pass the demon has performed a life changing, body and soul, conversion on you. Gout is so bad that it hurts me even to talk about it. After that first warning twinge, the demon leaps into bed with you, leans over your leg, and stabs you in that same big toe with an icepick. You cannot see him but you will never forget him. An icepick stabbed directly into the center of your big toe, right through the toenail, creates a horrible and indelible memory. You may forget birthdays, anniversaries and important business meetings but you will never forget the demon with the icepick. You will become a world class believer. You will call on the

Lord for mercy with the biggest megaphones and bull horns money can buy. Your entire neighborhood will become your personal confessional booth and all your neighbors will hear about your endless sinning! You will even make up sins to confess.

To sum up the pain of gout, over the years, we have collected the following quotes from old friends:

Good Quote - "When you have gout, you don't want the sheet to touch it."

Better Quote - "When you have gout, you don't want a breeze to blow on it."

Best Quote – "When you have gout, you don't even want a flashlight to shine on it."

Gout can hit you in almost any joint. Elbows and knees are especially painful. Some places on the foot are not as painful as others but if the Toe-Demon gets his hands on you and you don't choose to kill yourself, you will rank right up there on the tough guy scale with hockey goalies. If you have never had an attack of the gout, don't go looking for it. Watch your diet closely and know what causes uric acid to collect in all that fat and lard you have accumulated the past few years. Do your homework. Eat and drink the right things. There's a lot of good info out there about the gout, what causes it, how to prevent it and what meds you need to get from your doctor if you are attacked by it. Do not invite the gout to come and live with you!

Another unwelcome disorder (aren't they all?) that I have suffered for many years is peripheral neuropathy or PN for short. PN occurs when you lose the myelin sheath that normally covers and protects your nerves. The resulting pain is more bothersome to me than anything else but some people claim it causes burning pain, mainly in their feet. My pain is usually a stabbing knife like shock through parts of one foot or the other. They never both hurt at the same time. Believe it or not my feet are usually numb but when a pain strikes, I can certainly feel it. I have also lost my sense of touch or tactile perception in my fingers. I notice I tend to drop sheets of paper or other smaller objects I should be aware I am holding, however, I'm still keeping my grip on paper money pretty good! I know it's contradictory to say your feet are numb and they pain you at the same time but peripheral neuropathy can make that claim a good one.

PN is usually a disorder that diabetics suffer. I am not a diabetic. Doctors think my problem was caused from one or several of the medications I have taken over the years. I can only pray that my case is pretty much an arrested one. If I get any worse I am going to be wobbling into the furniture and bouncing off the walls. Maybe Katie Mae can get some kind of laser beam that she can strap to my head that has high volume vocal warnings built into the system. I just need a single loud warning word like, "WALL" or "DOOR" when I get out of line. I think that would be more humane than the electric cattle prod I saw her eyeing at the hardware store.

Biggest Loser? When You Race Your Fat And It Gains On You!

When you get my age and you are still mostly male it doesn't much matter anymore if you are pretty or not. However, if you have started giving a little thought to hanging around a few more years so you can watch the world go completely to hell then you might also think about all that excess fat meat you are hauling around. If you're like me you are just a big taxicab for a bunch of freeloading pounds that have been riding in the cheap seats. Unfortunately, we will ultimately pay the total fare for the free ride our big butts have been getting.

We have been creeping along at an old snail's pace but we've still managed to blow January totally off the 2013 calendar. Now it's a big blank in my memory. I want to try to take a slower approach in February so I don't get stressed mentally or physically. Katie Mae questions me in a calm, kindly, motherly voice, "If all your nerve endings are dead and you lost your mind in 1963, how can you be stressed anywhere?" A woman's logic always baffles me.

Anyhow, I know I have to look pretty good, in a manner of speaking, when I wear my Valentine's outfit and the third day after Valentine's, she would like for me to look suitably alive for her birthday. I was thinking of, "Spiffy," but I remembered last year when she and Paul took a look at me and said the word should be "Spoofy, and it rhymes with Goofy."

Stress makes you want to body slam people standing between you and the kitchen, (that's where we keep our refrigerator). We all know stress makes us pig out. If you perceive you are going through tough times or if you think hard times are just around the corner, your food choice is going to be high calorie. Binge-dieting women generally weigh 50 pounds more than women who diet using a consistent and peaceful program. I am trying to stress…..less stress!!

So I'm going for the easy. I just read another weird diet about how you can make vegetables so attractive that you will not want to eat them; you will hate to destroy the lovely veggie arrangements. But seriously, this diet makes you work! I can't believe a diet that makes you work is going to help the problem. By the time you peel and chop all those vegetables, you are going to be so hungry that you will eat everything you had stored in your vegetable bin. This diet had you preparing all kinds of veggies and then preparing this wonderful, delicate, lighter than air sauce to dip them in. Or you could have a spinach, celery or Vidalia onion smoothie. That is work! You can't lose weight if you're doing a lot of work in the kitchen. You have to eat a lot more calories in order to be able to do so much preparing and cooking! Kitchen work is hard work!!

My suggestion is to take it easy on your new diet. Don't hurt yourself. The diet is really no good if you kill yourself working to maintain it.

Here are several hints and tips I recently picked up on dieting and weight loss. They were given to me and they are yours for the taking. Just don't get stressed:

Do not try to lose weight by eating donut holes. Donut holes have no calories but eating your way through the donut to get to the hole can turn you into a vast waist land.

You can still count a banana split as a salad if you put a whole wheat crouton on the top and eat it all at one time while standing or while dining with someone you really like who is eating the same treat. You can keep the cherry but you have to take it home with you and eat it for breakfast Sunday morning.

There is a new miracle spice that you can eat that will literally burn the calories away, or so at least one hundred spammers have told me through e-mails. Beware. This is a trick. We do not need anything else to eat. We are trying to lose weight. You cannot eat yourself slim. I suggest you try the, "Sighted Weight Loss Program." Under this plan, you sit and stare at a picture of food that you really like. Start about 5:00 PM and continue to stare at it right through the 11:00 o'clock news. It works. Eventually you will pass out and when you wake, it will be time for breakfast.

Be sure you use a photograph. I tried it with a can of creamed corn and when I fell asleep, I dropped the can. It almost broke the big toe on my right foot. It hurt for a good three minutes before I decided to eat the corn to make my toe feel better.

My best plan yet is to find this gal I just read about who holds the world record for the largest hips. Her hips are eight feet in circumference. She is described as being "plus sized." I don't know where they got that description but calling eight foot hips "plus" defies all the math I was ever taught. That could not be a plus (+) for addition. This gal warrants the King's X for multiplication. She is ten times the definition of fat. I am going to become her close friend. As long as I can be around her, I am going to look so slim I'll never have to worry about dieting again.

I may have to break down and exercise a little. A friend just sent this to me and I think there might be a smidgen of truth somewhere in the good doctor's line. The doctor is speaking to his patient and asks him:

"What fits your busy schedule best? Would you rather exercise one hour per day or be dead twenty four hours per day?"

When Did Clementines Become "Cuties?"

I'm pretty upset with people who are constantly changing our words and adding new words and abbreviating the hell out of every good word we ever had. Nowadays it is not politically correct to cuss but don't worry if you tend to become blasphemous because these so called wordsmiths will take a long line of beautifully strung-together cuss words and change them into one long acronym that totally destroys the effectiveness of the curse you use to mentally flog a real or imagined enemy.

It will come out like, "GYMDNFSGASESOSB," and that wouldn't scare a small child, much less a 93 year old grandmotherly antagonist. It will not scare anybody! All this really makes me so mad because this word changing foolishness can kill an old guy. It's enormously dangerous to our health.

You will say that I am over reacting to something that isn't a big problem but let me tell you how this stupidity can cost you your life.

Katie Mae gave me a short grocery list on Wednesday. Wednesday was the day the big storms wiped out parts of North Georgia. Luckily we are a little south of where all the bad weather was hammering towns like Blairsville but I left early for the store because of the impending bad weather and I was a little rushed to keep from getting caught by wind and rain if it should come our way.

We had to have fruit. We have become convinced fruit will melt the excess lard from our less than svelte frames. We honestly believe some bright day we will once again be able to see our feet when we are standing.

So I took a quick trip down to Wal-Mart. Katie Mae had Cuties on her list of fruit. I did not know that Clementines were now called Cuties. We live in Athens so with Cuties at the top of my list it was fairly easy to pick up three UGA coeds. They were so cute. I thought it was too bad I couldn't show them off in a red and black convertible. Katie Mae did not think they were cute. As protection I had kept the grocery list just in case there was a misunderstanding but it didn't help at all.

I'm glad it was a short list because by the time I dug it out of my right nostril I had a terrible time getting those Cuties back to Wal-Mart. It was hard to see with so many tears in my eyes. I'd like to think I was sad and crying because I had to give up the girls. I suspect the real reason for the tears was severe spousal nostril abuse.

I cannot begin to tell you how cold, wet and windy it was trying to sleep on the deck Wednesday night during the storm. I was also harshly warned that getting that bed sheet she gave me dirty would mean real trouble.

I wonder if UGA has any free classes for old geezers who desperately need to learn new words and acronyms. I wonder if they know Clementines are called Cuties these days.

V – SOCIAL ISSUES

Social Issues is a catch-all name for whatever seems to blow my skirt up at any given moment. I try to stay away from politics, religion and the more colorful stories from my past for fear of shocking people older than me. I realize the crowd of people older than me is getting pretty slim but, thank God, there are still a good many of them around. They are much wiser and they are living longer. They may yet have a last futile chance to teach me a smidgen of the meaning of life. More importantly, I need to understand what the phrase, "what have you," means. The reason I bring it up is I keep thinking of this as a "what have you" category of stories. I understand "what have you," is an archaic phrase. I believe it perfectly describes a large number of today's social issues. I'm not sure I have labeled them correctly but here is my "what have you" group of social issues.

Who Begat John Wayne?

Who begat John Wayne?

I used begat because I was afraid if I asked, "Who made John Wayne?" I would be accused of saying John Wayne was a "Made Man," like in the mafia.

Surely our All American Hero of the Great Plains was sired by one of the premier western movie stars who came before him. His Daddy would have to be William S. Hart, Hoot Gibson or Tom Mix. But no, no, it was none of the above. Hang with me because the shock will be tremendous when you learn the unlikely source of John Wayne, the solid rock foundation of our youthful development.

Remember all the western movies where the good guy wins and the bad guy, or more likely, a heap of bad guys bite the gritty dust? We were fascinated. We were mesmerized. The western movies made us into the many good citizens and maybe a few bad apples we later became. John Wayne did that to us. We are all spiritually cloaked by the "John Wayne Syndrome."

He was the epitome of the real man. He was tough, hard as a slab of granite with a heart as large as a longhorn steer's. He had courage, tenacity, honesty, integrity and all-of-the above plus much, much more all rolled up like a solid tumble weed into one big man. We loved him. We were him and he was us. We still are him. We can't shake that persona.

So who turned Marion Robert Morrison into John Wayne and changed our lives forever? Here's how it all happened to us and it is the fault of Theodore Roosevelt, Henry Cabot Lodge and William Randolph Hearst.

Roosevelt would go on to become the 26th president of the USA. Lodge was a United States congressman in the House of Representatives and later in the US Senate from 1887 to 1924. Hearst was also a US Congressman but is most noted as an American newspaper publisher who built the nation's largest newspaper chain.

According to Evan Thomas in his most interesting book, "The War Lovers," in 1898 Roosevelt, Lodge and Hearst were hell-bent on getting the United States into a war with Spain. They were all terribly disappointed because the sun was slowly setting in the west over the last great frontier for men of action. There were no more Indians to fight. There was no place these hardy lads could go to hear the boom of cannon and experience the thrill of a cavalry chase. They were fearless warriors with no place to wage war.

Who gave them the notion they were fearless warriors? The truth is they were all upper crust Easterners. They met at Harvard and were all members of The Porcellian Club which had only about twenty members and its only practical use was to provide them a forum for dining and heavy drinking. I suspect each of them was living in the shadow of his father whose strong presence cast a pall over any dreams, hopes and ambitions of the son. They were forever doomed to strive to prove their prowess and manliness to their fathers. Roosevelt was quoted as saying the only man he ever feared was his father.

Today in our society these three would appear to be foppish dandies or sissies. They were certainly different and peculiar. Even Roosevelt who later became president continued to project his manly demeanor all over the globe by killing thousands of wild animals and he appeared to always be trying to prove his manliness. There is no question he was a brilliant Renaissance man who could hold forth on practically any subject.

Lodge was born in the highest of Boston Brahmin blue blood snobbery. His Mother was a Cabot. The old Boston toast or poem (a variation) to their social standing goes:

And this to good old Boston

The home of the bean and the cod.

Where the Lodges talk to the Cabots

And the Cabots speak only to God.

Hearst was the creator of "Yellow Journalism." Many of the stories published by his papers were manufactured to create sensationalism and to sell papers. Nowadays he is most widely known for being the main character depicted in Orson Welles' classic movie, "Citizen Kane." His political power was derived from his ownership of thirty newspapers in the US and he was expertly adroit at wielding his power of the press.

Roosevelt was a Republican who became the leader of the Progressive (Bull Moose) Party. He seemed to be a liberal Republican except when it came to war and killing large animals with high-powered rifles. He was forty years old when he insisted on using his political pull to get him in the US Army so he could join in the battle with the cavalry in making a mad dash up San Juan Hill in Cuba during the Spanish American War of 1898. That was his only year of military service. He longed to be a cowboy and his rambunctiousness was almost certainly curtailed, in a good and positive way by his wife, Edith.

To make a long story short, as it should be because it is so sad when you lose a hero like John Wayne, our three war lovers had a confederate in the Porcellian Club by the name of Owen Wister. A few years after they had all left Harvard, Roosevelt, Hearst and Lodge were busy stirring up our war with Spain after the American ship USS Maine was blown up in Havana Harbor. It probably was blown up by an on-board accident but the war lovers would have none of that explanation. Immediately employing every political resource they could muster, they blamed Spain for the explosion and Teddy got his golden opportunity to charge up San Juan Hill astride a galloping steed in a full blown cavalry charge. Cuba has never been the same.

If Owen Wister does not ring a bell with you, don't worry. You know I'm duty bound to tell you about him. While the war lovers were stifling their boredom by engaging in stirring up a needless war between the USA and Spain, Owen Wister was attacking the same brand of boredom in his own unique way.

Wister's father had him working in New York as a bank clerk. The story goes that Wister went west for his health which may be true but some people say Owen was tired of sitting at a desk in an office in New York City and after one visit to Medicine Bow, Wyoming, he was ruined forever. He fell totally in love with the great outdoors and the life of the cowboy.

The only trouble was the cowboy was much maligned in those days. The cowboy was lowly, nasty, unkempt, unshaven, cowardly, despicable, universally unpopular (and also not liked very much) until Owen Wister appeared on the scene.

And then in 1902 Owen Wister changed it all. The old Harvard Porcellian Club imbiber magically turned the lowly unloved cowboy into the Great American Hero that he has remained to us for well over a hundred years. Owen Wister wrote "The Virginian."

"The Virginian" has been made into a movie four times and a fifth time it was revised into a "made for television" movie. It was also the long running television series that we so much enjoyed from 1962 to 1971 that starred James Drury,

Doug McClure and Lee J. Cobb. "The Virginian" made famous a line that we have all heard before but bears repeating here. During a poker game, one player called the sheriff an SOB. The sheriff looked at the fellow and said, "When you call me that, smile." Wister had his hero repeat that line in his book.

There were short stories and pulp dime novels about the Old West before "The Virginian" but never a novel of such scope and force. One year later, in 1903, the first Western Cowboy movie was filmed. The movie maker was The Edison Film Company and it was shot on a budget of $150.00. "The Great Train Robbery" was twelve minutes long and was a silent shoot 'em up with the bad guys robbing passengers on a train and then being chased by a posse of good guys who wiped out all the bad guys. The star was Broncho Billy Anderson.

And thus was born our love for cowboys, all the great old cowboy stars led by John Wayne who has been called, "The Bearer of Moral Absolutes." This was the birth of the mythical Old West we still embrace and if you missed it because you are so young, I feel sorry for you but the beauty of today's media allows you to seek it out and watch every minute of it. These were great stories of cowboys and Indians and lawmen and bandits.

So there you have it. I maintain that Owen Wister and his Harvard college swells created our hero, John Wayne. You can almost say that Owen Wister was John Wayne's daddy. I know it was not Broncho Billy Anderson and at 5'2" Buzz

Barton was too short. He was the shortest cowboy star. Besides he was six years younger than John Wayne.

I could go on forever but I have to go downstairs and practice my gangly, gimpy sidewinder kind of walk up to the mirror, cock my head to one side and drawl, "Listen Pilgrim, and listen good!"

Giving Doomsters the Dump!

I don't know about you but I'm pretty weary of getting six or eight e-mails every week from some group of whackos who want to sell me miscellaneous expert survival guides and tools. I wonder about the age of such idiots and how old they may be. I don't know about these jerks but I'm into my 71st year and I think I know a little bit about surviving.

There is a serious backlash from some of those Mayan calendar flakes who are somewhere rubber-rooming and bouncing off the walls like frantic slinkies in their own strange world of freaky suspense. They are wigged out because we are all still here, living, laughing and kicking; December 21, 2012 passively arrived and sleepily left. Now it is just another date on last year's calendar.

The Mayan calendar failed us. We were supposed to be wiped out in a cataclysmic upheaval of gigantic proportions and the dooms-dayers are bitching and moaning because we were not smashed to smithereens and we are not now hurtling through space at two hundred light years per second. It is not a big secret that the beginning of the Mayan calendar was based on a mythical creation date. The Mayans and their calendar never mentioned anything about the end of the world or great earthly changes on December 21, 2012. They left those kinds of ignorant predictions for twenty first century morons.

It never stops! I remember in 1989 I had a truck driver and dispatcher I worked with tell me that in 1990 the world was coming to an end and to back up that promise they had two or three hundred reprints of a book that foretold the end of the world in 1990. I had truck drivers afraid to drive from Atlanta to Birmingham because they were scared they would drive off the edge of the earth. Many drivers were frightened. I had to sit them all down and rip the new cover off one of the books to show them the damned thing had first been published and printed in 1890. It was a hundred years old. The world did not end in 1890 and it was not going to end in 1990. I took care of the remainder of the books. Sometimes burning books ain't all that bad.

We can never hope to patch all the cracks in the woodwork fast enough to keep these imbeciles from coming out of them. They come out of holes and from under rocks non-stop. But brace yourself and be strong. Keep your eye on them. There are multitudes of misguided people in this country and if you think this is a result of the dumbing down of America, you are wrong.

Many of these people are highly intelligent. That could be the problem. Colleges and Universities are turning out young people who are well read but only about certain subjects. Most have never cracked a history book since high school and few of them have the basics in walking around sense.

This is the scary part. There is a Doomsday Clock at the University of Chicago. It has been there since 1947. It is not a perpetual clock but the intellectual egghead reasoning for having such a clock is perpetual. It's perpetually stupid. It's set to tell us when the world is going to self-destruct, with our help of course. In 1947 the hands were set at seven minutes until midnight. As you might guess, the last second before midnight is your last chance to blink before imminent destruction and doom descends on our hapless heads. Seven minutes until midnight was decided on because by 1945 we had developed, created and used the atomic bomb. In later years, when the cold war was over, the minute hand was moved back to show 17 minutes until midnight.

Now the clock is at five minutes until midnight because 2012 was a brutal year with extended droughts, horrible hurricanes like Sandy, chemical and biological scares and nuclear disasters. So 2013 is the year. Yep, we're in it again. We're going to get wiped and swiped this year. I'm telling you, it never ends with this crowd of Bozo's.

Now to ease your mind a bit, I'm going to take certain matters in hand and see if we can take some of that pressure off you. I have seen a picture of that clock at the University of Chicago and I believe that minute hand is just the right size to be of great use to us.

I have chosen Bubba Jack Johnson to go with me because he is going to be our Perpetual Pollyanna. Bubba Jack is always friendly, happy and smiling. He has few sad days. We are going to find that clock and rip that totally offensive minute hand off its dark face. We are going to use that once obnoxiously offending hand as our own terrible, swift sword. To be merciful we'll use only the flat side of the blade to soundly smack the forehead of anyone who might feel inclined to warn us of impending doom. After we have beat their dumb asses into happy submission, we are going to find Chicken Little and beat his little tail until he chirps pessimistically no more.

If dooms day predictors are making you melancholy, just call me and Bubba Jack Johnson. We'll show them the serious flat side of that clock hand and then toss them into the nearest dumpster. Once a doomster has been dumpstered, his outlook improves. He becomes more cheerful when he finally gets out of the big trash bin and realizes life in the real world isn't so bad after all.

So cheer up! Be happy! There will not be a doomsday! Chicken Little is coming back South with us and we better not ever hear another sad peep out of him about the sky falling while we have our hands around his scrawny neck!

Reality Shows! Is There Such a Thing as Fictional Fact?

Did you know the first reality show on TV was Alan Funt's "Candid Camera" that first ran in 1948? Did you know, that now, there are so many reality shows, they can't be counted. One of my sources replied to the question, "How many reality shows are there" with the answer, "too damned many to count." Another source listed 6,876. They count all the shows like "American Idol" and "Dancing with the Stars" and each year's new production is added to the list as a separate reality show.

82 percent of viewers say reality shows are totally made up, mostly distorted and they are wearing out their welcome. Apparently the genre is falling apart and it is doomed, so soak it all in before it evaporates.

Different web sources will give you differing ranks of reality shows but I have listed a few here that I got from this website: WWW.imdb.com. I only talk about the ones that interest me and all my Southern blue-blooded redneck friends. Some of the rankings are intriguing in that they show you just how dumbed down we have become.

Some shows that are in trouble and in the courts being sued include "Whale Wars," (I'm not sure of the ranking); #15, "Keeping Up With the Kardashians;" #17, "Storage Wars;" #54, "Amish Mafia," and HGTV's "House Hunters," (not sure of rank).

"Whale Wars" is being sued for five million dollars for sinking a man's ship. The ship owner says the show misrepresented the state and condition of his ship and sabotaged it to encourage viewers to donate to The Sea Shepherds which is an anti-whaling group. "Keeping up with the Kardashians," has recently been accused of faking scenes. A picture said to be taken of Kris and Kim in Dubai in October was actually taken in an LA studio in December. The gals had the same outfits on or were seen with the same outfits in both photographs.

#17, "Storage Wars," is being sued by cast member, Dave Hester (Yuup, it's the Yuup guy) for either 750K or millions of dollars depending which news story you read. Hester says the show persists in, "illegal activity and deceiving the public." He says the show paid for plastic surgery of a cast member to hype up the sex appeal of the show. We are pretty sure plastic surgery money was not spent on Darrell Sheets or Barry Weiss. I like "Storage Wars" and the characters but if you watch this show and you think the events are real, you have a serious reality gap right in the middle of your empty head. Valuables are secreted in the storage rooms by the show's staff. Think about it!!! If someone was so broke they could not pay the storage fee for three months, and by California law the contents could be sold, do you think the cash poor property owners would leave something they could convert into money? At one time "Storage Wars" was A&E's most watched program, ever.

Lancaster, PA local police say that #54, "Amish Mafia," does not even exist and if you see a picture of the police rousting out members of the, "Amish Mafia," there are no police reports of detentions or arrests because they never happened. By the same token, HGTV's, "House Hunters" are actually showing houses that are not for sale and at least one house shown was, in reality, still occupied by the owners.

You might enjoy seeing the rankings listed below if you watch any of the reality shows.

#1 is either "Sunday Night Football" or "King of the Nerds." It's your choice and since the football season has fallen off the edge of the earth it must be "King of the Nerds." I've never heard of "King of the Nerds," and that's probably a healthy thing for my last three surviving brain cells.

#2 is "American Idol" (Wednesday nights) and when they make their choice of which singer stays and which one goes (Thursday nights), the second night show will rank between #4 and #6.

#4 is "Duck Dynasty," and it is immensely popular with just about every guy and gal I talk to down here in the sunny South. For that reason I would like to save my comments on "Duck Dynasty" for last.

#5: I've stuck "The Bachelor," in here so the girls can get an idea where this show ranks. I don't know any girls who care but there must be a legion of you ladies out there burning up your TV's on "The Bachelor" because you have shot that ranking through the roof.

#6 is one of my favorites. It's called "Pawn Stars." I like to see the strange items and antiques brought in to the pawn shop. I also enjoy "Antiques Roadshow" for the same reason. I love history and I love antiques. I enjoy the main man, Rick Harrison because he has no problem laughing at his own remarks. He amuses himself and I tend to do the same stupid thing. This is the show's sixth year and it will be lucky to make a seventh year because the show is beginning to turn from unlikely to unbelievable.

Some other shows I know you are dying to hear about include:

#13 "Honey Boo Boo." This reminds me of the days certain books were banned and it makes me think, "What's wrong with censorship?"

#23-"Gold Rush, Alaska," This is pretty interesting except commercials eat up 30% of the time you can actually see a show. That means you spend only about 40 to 45 minutes watching these guys and if they spent about 25 to 30 minutes trying to repair their old worn out mining equipment, you get very little quality gold-finding action. Something is broken or tears all to hell on every show.

"Teen Mom #2" is ranked #29 but if you are wondering why in the world we had to have a 'Teen Mom #2" you are right on the "real' reality track and there may be help for you in the "Real" world. Our teen mom #2 is apparently such a fruitcake the staff and producers cannot control this gal and there will be no new season. I know this breaks many hearts but you will just have to suck it up!

#34 "Hardcore Pawn," Believe it or not there are a heap of people out there willing to sit on their numb bums and watch this dysfunctional family bitch and moan at each other the entire show except when they are bitching and moaning with their, so-called, customers.

"Sons of Guns" is #35 - I threw this one in for my gun loving buddies.

"American Pickers" is #37- Can be, at times, interesting and, many times, boring as hell.

"Thc Voice" is #45 for those of you who enjoy it.

For you lovers of big trucks and tow trucks, I'm sure you'll be pleased to know that Lizard Lick Towing is #52. If you think this show is for real, please don't tell anybody. Your wife can save pertinent information like this and, one day, when she gets "Really, Really" tired of you and begins to see the "Real" you, this will help her immeasurably in having you committed. I know because I fell in love with Sonia on "Operation Repo" and I caught Katie Mae making notes about my viewing habits. I think she's building a case against me. A real let down for me was learning "Lizard Lick Towing" is #52 and my Sonia's show was only #161.

Don't give up. There's more but it also gets more and more disappointing to people who love their "Real" high on a scale of, "Unreal."

"Hoarders," is #77. If you like "Hoarders," you are undoubtedly living a super miserable life and you are way down in the reality trenches. Things will soon be looking up for you....because that's the only place you can go from watching "Hoarders."

For you swamp boys and fleshy headed ax men it's getting worse, or better, as the case may be. "Gator Boys" is #51; "Ax Men" is #59; "Dog the Bounty Hunter" is #64; "Swamp People" is #115; "Doomsday Preppers" is #173 and poor old "Bering Sea Gold, Under the Ice" is way down at #312. I think we should be able to go ahead and bomb the "Doomsday Preppers" off the face of the earth and we won't have to worry about them taking up valuable network time any more. Hell, it won't come as a surprise to them. They've been expecting it! They should be ready for it by now. We can keep their stuff because they won't need it anymore. They have been seeing this coming, like forever!

I saved #4 "Duck Dynasty" until last for a particular reason. I have a lot of friends and relatives who like "Duck Dynasty" and I think I know why. We all wish we could support half a dozen families or more while tubing in a pond out back or wandering around at night gigging poor defenseless frogs (maybe not you gals) or all piling into a motor home and riding down the road to get a hot dog or some ice cream without ever worrying about who's minding the store. This is so freaking unreal it's pathetic. Have you ever seen them make a duck call from start to finish? Have you ever seen any of them actually producing even a small box of duck calls? Have they ever gone out to a big lake and called in some ducks. I have not watched all their shows but I can bet, and probably win the bet, that the answer to all my questions is a big, resounding, "No!"

So why do we love them? It's because we are all from the South. I'm pretty sure I was in the fourth grade at Mulberry School in Albany, Georgia with Phil and Si Robertson back in 1951. Phil and Si had those long, gray beards in the fourth grade. I had a crush on a girl that looked like Jase. She also had a long beard in the fourth grade. We had a fourth grade teacher who could have been Willie's twin sister only her beard was a little lighter and a little longer.

Those guys are funny to us because we grew up with them. They have always been crazy as hell and nothing has changed them in all these years. Their lines are not usually that funny. That deadpan delivery makes them laughable. They'll never change.

Our old Junior High School principal, Mr. Paul Robertson, was some kin to those boys. He broke the mold by learning to talk good English. He went on to become an educator. I don't believe he ever made any duck calls but if he had, they would have been good'uns and he never slacked work like those Louisiana guys.

The only one that has got a damned lick of walking around sense is Miss Kay and those boys better take good care of her because they'll be lost without her.

They'll be just about as lost as I get when I start to wondering what ever happened to the television networks that gave us such good entertainment in the past. Where are our channels: National Geographic, The Discovery Channel, A&E and the History Channels? I'll tell you where they are. They are all showing this same gibberish that makes us even dumber than we were when we were at Mulberry Street School in the fourth grade.

Boy, if we could resurrect folks like Mr. Paul Robertson. Mr. Rob had a duck dynasty too. He could royally burn your ass if you didn't keep your ducks in a row.

Damning the Spamming!

I need some help here. The few hairs left on my head are 99.14% gray and when I look at myself in the mirror every morning, the color of my hair is my best reminder that I know next to nothing about computers. I don't think I really need to know much as long as we have all these bright young people around who can answer my dumb questions.

But spamming is a totally different question. The young and brave of heart seem just as frustrated, confused and generally mad as hell as I am when I see spammy crap all over my monitor every day that has nothing to do with me. We absolutely must have a way to get back at these nut cases who continually waste our time. We are spending the better part of our lives dealing with pure junk that leaves us miserable and sick of having to look at something we do not want to see and did not invite into our cozy cloud.

Where are all the bright young minds that can help us? It would be fun to be able to spam spammers right back with a double dose of clutter as soon as they start clogging our airwaves with rubbish but all I really need is for some of y'all (y'all is Southern for y'all) to tell me how to get my hands on them.

I'm aware you already know this but let me go ahead and tell you why:

I turned 71 in November. I do not really need three shoe boxes full of Viagra. I do not want to spend even the twelve cents for the packaging. I do not want any Viagra. I want to live a bit longer. Using Viagra to extend my life is not an option for me.

I do not want a Chinese wife. I do not want a Russian wife. I do not want to meet some woman under 50. I have a wife and her age is over 50 and her age is fine with me. She's a buzz saw that I can't begin to keep up with so why would I need two of them. Even if I could get a new one who is only 50, I thought I just made it clear that I would like to live a little longer. I don't want to meet any young Christian women and, more importantly, I do not want to meet any women who are heathens, young or old.

I am sick of seeing my financial status simultaneously skyrocket and plummet. I am getting tired of seeing hundreds of offers of loans for weird sums ranging from $1,016.00 to $1533.00.

I have been warned many thousands of times that the new auto insurance laws in Georgia will allow me to insure seven vehicles for four dollars a year. After the warnings are issued, follow-up e-mails harshly chastise me for not heeding the first forty thousand warnings.

I used to like Dr. Oz but if I get one more message from him about trying out his diet plan, I'm having a doll made in his likeness by a local Hatian voodoo guru. The price includes six long sharp jabbing needles. Old Doc Oz is going to need a new cure. You'll see him begging for relief on "The Doctors'" show.

The huge insult these despicable pieces of trash pile on to the vast heap of injury they deliver us daily is.....none of the illiterate bastards can spell or type. I just got one that says, "Disappointed with sexual helath?" I've got to be truthful here. I think I have always been disappointed with my sexual helath I showed this to Katie Mae and she said, "That's health dumbo. They misspelled it." I did not tell her I thought it was Italian for somehow getting the heels of your feet involved in a sexual act. I don't think she could have handled the thought.

So now if you young problem solvers can bring these people out of the cracks in the woodwork and go to work on them the outpouring of gratitude from the masses would be mind boggling. No telling how fast your financial status would skyrocket.

Why can't you develop a fairly nonviolent program like the one the gamers are always using to blow their enemies to smithereens? I can see the spammer's dirty words being machine gunned into tiny bits with the letters to each word falling into pieces smaller than confetti at their very own feet before he or she can even get a word off.

If that is too violent and not politically correct for some people, how about rounding up a few spammers and bring them to me? The effect will be the same. When I get through with five or six of them (I tire easily) I'll let the rest go. The word will spread like wildfire. I'm old. I still believe in corporal punishment. I have an iron post out back that I can chain them to. I will cane their sorry asses to within an inch of their worthless lives. There will be no more spammers on the East Coast. You folks out west can just go ahead and shoot the ones we send you. I know most of you are like me and don't give much of a damn about whether to be PC or not to be PC.

CPSIA information can be obtained
at www.ICGtesting.com
Printed in the USA
LVOW13s0026280217
525610LV00013B/765/P